PRAISE FOR
THE COTTAGE SCHOOL MODEL

TCS is the kind of school that all schools should be. Many of my clients were failing, depressed, being suspended from school, or otherwise not learning and thriving until they started attending TCS, where they soared. Considering the brilliance, wisdom, and passion of its founders, TCS could not have been anything other than the remarkable success it is today.

—Chris Vance

Special Education/Disability Law Attorney

I am hesitant to say anything because I don't want to jinx it, but Sam's behavior is nothing short of miraculous. There was a time last year when I started to lose faith. It didn't look like he was going to make it, but clearly something changed for the better.

The child is doing work with no parental intervention. He is packed every day. He is getting up, getting dressed, and even asked to go in early yesterday to work with one of his teachers because he was a bit confused about Macbeth.

Wow! Sam is more confident, more responsible, and a better student than he ever was in public school. I'm a true believer. Count me in as one of the converts. You guys rock!

—TCS Parent

TCS takes differentiated instruction to a completely elevated level. I have seen students with significant learning disabilities instructed alongside gifted students. Yet, each student's needs are fully met. Unlike other schools, every student who attends TCS must have a graduation plan prior to receiving their diploma. As a result, the alumni I have met are all fully productive members of society. The students who choose to go to college are well prepared for the rigor and those who choose not to attend college become gainfully employed. The Digiesos have provided a structure and created an environment that promotes learning, self-advocacy, and successful transition into the next phase of the student's life.

—Dr. Bonnie Cohen-Greenberg

THE COTTAGE SCHOOL MODEL

THE BREAKTHROUGH
EDUCATIONAL PARADIGM FOR
REAL-LIFE LEARNING

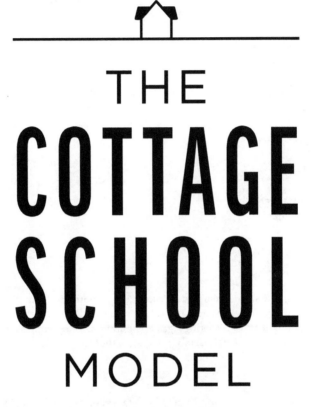

THE
COTTAGE
SCHOOL
MODEL

JOSEPH DIGIESO, M.ED.
JACQUE DIGIESO, PH.D.

Published by Advantage, Charleston, South Carolina.
Member of Advantage Media Group.

ADVANTAGE is a registered trademark, and the Advantage colophon is a trademark of Advantage Media Group, Inc.

Printed in the United States of America.

10 9 8 7 6 5 4 3 2 1

ISBN: 978-1-642250-66-4
LCCN: 2019940403

Cover design by Carly Blake.
Layout design by Megan Elger.

This publication is designed to provide accurate and authoritative information in regard to the subject matter covered. It is sold with the understanding that the publisher is not engaged in rendering legal, accounting, or other professional services. If legal advice or other expert assistance is required, the services of a competent professional person should be sought.

Advantage Media Group is proud to be a part of the Tree Neutral® program. Tree Neutral offsets the number of trees consumed in the production and printing of this book by taking proactive steps such as planting trees in direct proportion to the number of trees used to print books. To learn more about Tree Neutral, please visit **www.treeneutral.com**.

Advantage Media Group is a publisher of business, self-improvement, and professional development books and online learning. We help entrepreneurs, business leaders, and professionals share their Stories, Passion, and Knowledge to help others Learn & Grow. Do you have a manuscript or book idea that you would like us to consider for publishing? Please visit **advantagefamily.com** or call **1.866.775.1696**.

To Steven and Eric, our beloved sons.
To the students and their families who struggle with
school/social success.

TABLE OF CONTENTS

ACKNOWLEDGMENTS

We would like to acknowledge the following:

The many families who entrusted their precious children to us and who partnered with us as we guided each student toward their dreams.

The professionals who shared their specific expertise with our staff and families and advised us along the way.

The community partners who provided resources and served as ambassadors for our unique educational approach.

Our board of directors who guided us through the years of challenges and celebrations.

Our family who steadfastly believed in our dream, encouraged us always, and often sacrificed family times together when school obligations prevailed.

ABOUT THE AUTHORS

Joe Digieso began his career in education forty years ago after deciding to leave his position as a management consultant for Beatrice Foods. Once his wife talked him into tutoring students, he discovered that he loved teaching and sacrificed a promising career as an executive to return to school to obtain a master's degree in education. His teaching experience began in Dekalb County, Georgia, and he was selected as one of the two teachers to open one of Georgia's first alternative schools, Hamilton Alternative. The school catered to students whose behavioral problems prevented them from attending home schools. Joe spent five years teaching and serving as an administrator at an independent school for students with learning disabilities, now called Mill Springs Academy. He cofounded The Educational Resource Center, a tutorial center in 1983; and The Cottage School in 1985, where he has served as an instructor, the high school principal, the middle school principal, and the treasurer of the Cottage School board of directors.

Jacque Digieso, PhD, has taught in Arkansas, Thailand, Ohio, and Georgia in both public and private settings. Every classroom added to her commitment to create an environment of acceptance, safety, and growth. She has served in leadership positions in her church, was the president in her local Rotary Club, and the president of Atlanta Area Association of Independent Schools. She is a Fulbright Memorial Fund recipient, has been named Business Diva by Atlanta Business to Business, was nominated for Woman of the Year by *Atlanta Woman's Magazine*, and was named Phenomenal Woman of North Fulton, and Outstanding Georgia Citizen. She and Joe were awarded the Small Business Persons of the Year award by the Greater North Fulton Chamber of Commerce. Jacque and Joe have been married for fifty years. They have two sons and five grandchildren.

FOREWORD

In 1985, when The Cottage School was founded, Joe and Jacque Digieso felt strongly that traditional education was not prepared to effectively educate students who learned differently. Specifically, they were concerned that teens with attention deficit disorder (ADD) were often misunderstood and left behind. Students' creativity, heightened energy, and curiosity were challenges in traditional school classroom environments.

The Digiesos recognized early on that students with ADD had qualities which, if harnessed correctly, could be productive and help them excel in the workplace. Serving these students, and looking ahead to bright future possibilities for them, led Joe and Jacque to begin The Cottage School.

Not long after the school's founding, the Digiesos were looking to expand. They wanted to move it from a small house to a nineteen-acre property on Grimes Bridge Road, which was on the real estate market and represented by my business. As president of Northside Reality, I was glad to meet with the Digiesos and help broker the sale. The rest is history.

Their growing school provides the traditional state-approved academic curriculum, but in a setting that is organized as if the students were in a job setting. The structure includes a business casual dress code, two-week academic planners, and a mock salary system for responsible behaviors—an incentive program that encourages participation. Combined with a robust extracurricular model that includes carpentry, horticulture, auto mechanics, arts, music, athletics, and leisure skills, The Cottage School model prepares students for the working world, post-secondary academics, and community activism.

Alumni have found success in all walks of life. From two Grammy winners, to teachers, doctors, attorneys, inventors, authors, chefs, and small-business owners, they are successful and productive members of their communities.

Since its creation in 1985, and thanks to its dedicated staff and teachers, The Cottage School has been recognized as one of the top fifty schools in the nation serving students who learn differently. The Digiesos have shared their techniques and stories at national conferences. In this book, they share their stories with the reader.

I'm so glad that their property purchase was fruitful and I'm glad to be a very small part of their story. I wish them continued success.

—Senator Johnny Isakson

LISTENING TO THE UNIVERSE

*There are no extra pieces in the universe. Everyone
is here because he or she has a place to fill, and every
piece must fit itself into the big jigsaw puzzle.*

—Deepak Chopra

When we started our life together, one of us, Jacque (pronounced
"Jackie"), was an educator, and one of us, Joe, was a business person.[1]
We had no idea that we would one day decide to create the renowned
special-needs school model—The Cottage School (TCS)—which
we first conceived in 1981 and then devoted the larger part of our
lives to. Even in 1985 after we established the campus on nineteen
beautiful acres along the Chattahoochee River Corridor in Roswell,
Georgia,[2] we could not foresee that it would become a first choice

---

1   For the sake of expediency, rather than switch narration back and forth between
     us, we will simply refer to ourselves in third person where needed, throughout
     this book.

2   The Cottage School campus now comprises twenty-three acres.

for special-needs education in the Atlanta region. We certainly did not predict it would be named a Top 50 Best Private Special Needs School in the United States.[3]

To us, the real-world methodology that forms the "scaffold" of TCS was the logical takeaway from the many years each of us spent educating both mainstream students and children with unique learning challenges. Those special needs ran the gamut from neurologically based to situationally generated and beyond. In our early teaching years, such needs had largely been unaddressed by both public and private education.

WHAT MOTIVATED US TO CREATE TCS?

The fact is, back in the 1970s and '80s, many neurologically based learning disorders had not been identified or properly classified by the *DSM* (*Diagnostic and Statistical Manual of Mental Disorders*). Consequently, children with unique learning needs were routinely shuffled in and out of mainstream schools as conventional educators were faced with students they could not effectively serve. Parents struggled to find educational professionals who could identify the potential in their children and help them make their way in a complex world. Very few of those professionals existed at the time, because the science around the neurology had not fully emerged. What's more, because so many learning challenges had not been identified as neurologically based, the scope of the need resembled an iceberg—most of it was concealed beneath the surface of society, resulting in a constellation of unrecognized "unique" learning needs.

---

3   "The 50 Best Private Special Needs Schools in the United States," The Masters in Special Education Program Guide, accessed March 7, 2019, https://www.masters-in-special-education.com/50-best-private-special-needs-schools/2014.

Schools were simply not equipped to address learning needs that deviated from the main teaching highway; many are not, even today. In our early years working in conventional schools with what were sometimes termed "unteachable" students, it was not uncommon for us to be told to "just keep them out of trouble." For this, and many other reasons, we found our calling in defying the teaching prognoses around even the most severely learning-challenged students. As each year went by, we were more determined to prove that *all* young people, learning-challenged or not, could learn and thrive, uncover their talents and passions, and make full and rich lives for themselves in what otherwise might have seemed a hostile world. We were listening to our universe.

As each year went by, we were more determined to prove that all young people, learning-challenged or not, could learn and thrive, uncover their talents and passions, and make full and rich lives for themselves.

Years later, we admitted that we were never surprised by the dramatic results we were able to achieve through our real life-based, individualized educational model, even if our students and families sometimes were! What did surprise us was how rapidly our student body grew and how quickly we had to scramble in those early years to keep up with the need while we kept the venture of our lives and hearts going.

TCS TODAY

Now, thirty-plus years after The Cottage School was founded, we speak with educators and parents, and help them recreate the TCS educational solution for their students and children, whether it involves

- trailblazing new types of learning delivery in their existing public and independent schools;

- starting their own home-schooling, cooperative teaching, blended or embedded program initiatives; or

- launching a full-scale special-needs or independent school in their area.

From its humble beginnings in an office park, The Cottage School has attracted inquiries from educators and parents all over the country who seek to deliver more effective and meaningful education. We believe that this is because the TCS method provides education that does what education is *supposed* to do: help every young person fulfill their true potential as a confident, productive, and independent adult. TCS "unlocks the box" that so many learning-challenged young people find themselves in, within more conventional educational environments. "We teach differently," is how we often explain our success.

With its balanced blend of individualized, experiential, and academic programming for grades four to twelve, the proven Cottage School method has unquestionably transformed the lives of students with unique learning needs.

WE ARE ALL "UNIQUE NEEDS" LEARNERS

The two of us could not have known at the outset that the school we created for learning disabled (LD) students in the mid-1980s would also become an award-winning[4] model for better educating *any* young person. It turns out that all students who move through an

---

4   In June 2014, the *Masters in Special Education Resource Guide* named The Cottage School one of its 50 Best Private Special Needs Schools in the United States.

educational system have "unique" needs. *Every* individual has a special style of learning. Each human being has a distinct way of seeing, comprehending, and learning about the world. We filter our intake of the world through our personal and family life situations and through our body chemistry and our neurology. (In the case of learning, neurological challenges can impact the ability to receive, process, store, and respond to auditory, visual, or spatial information.) Often, we are thwarted in our learning by roadblocks no one else can see.

All students who move through an educational system have "unique" needs. Every individual has a special style of learning.

So, the question that the two of us came up against, again and again, as we made our way through our life together was: Why should any young person be prevented from fulfilling their purpose, just because the conventional educational system as it exists today doesn't "speak" to them? Furthermore, we wondered: Does an individual's need for a learning structure that differs from what is considered mainstream teaching mean that they are less talented, less innately intelligent, less motivated, less determined to succeed, or less able to learn?

We knew that couldn't be so. After all, Albert Einstein was famously the poster child for young people who faced unique learning challenges. Depending on the information source, Einstein is reported to have talked late and reluctantly, was unable to memorize material (a requirement in the day), and demonstrated a reading disability. Some now say he probably suffered from dyslexia and Asperger's syndrome; others suggest he may have exhibited traits of schizophrenia. Einstein's early instructors considered him "dull-witted." But more recent experts argue that, in a generation that was required to learn by rote, young Einstein was simply unfortunate to have possessed a mind given to creative reasoning and out-of-the-box thinking.[5] The result was that, for Einstein, the puzzle pieces of learner and teaching system simply did not fit together.

There have been many other figures of astounding achievement who are reported to have struggled with learning: Galileo, Mozart, Thomas Edison, Woodrow Wilson, General George Patton, George Bernard Shaw, Prince Charles, Robert Kennedy, and Nelson Rockefeller. More recent are Henry Belafonte, Charles Schwab, Dustin Hoffman, Henry Winkler, Tom Cruise, and Magic Johnson.

Somehow, all of these amazing people—through sheer grit and determination—managed to burn their own detours around an orthodox teaching system and invent unique wheels of learning that worked for them. In effect, they created their own learning systems to keep them moving toward their visions of who and what they could be. Our own experience as educators tells us that as these individuals came up against the inevitable roadblocks, it may have been their eye-on-the-prize that kept them striving. Somehow, as they were repeatedly knocked down (the story most people with unique learning needs share), they recovered their inspiration to rise up and try once more.

Were all of these people fortunate enough to have a parent or mentor continually inspire them to learn in a world not conducive to their needs? We may never know, and we may never know why these particular individuals made their way so successfully in the world when so many others could not.

---

5   Barbara Wolff and Hananya Goodman, "The Legend of the Dull-Witted Child Who Grew Up to Be a Genius," The Hebrew University of Jerusalem, February 2016, http://www.albert-einstein.org/article_handicap.html.

WHAT SHOULD LEARNING DO FOR US?

What we do know is that far too many young people, especially those with more evident learning disabilities, struggle to succeed within the educational system as it currently exists. It is also fair to say, since our nation's schools acknowledge it, that there is a percentage of students in almost every school that does not meet the learning "norm." In the US, although the high school graduation rate has recently climbed to 84 percent, about 17 percent of high school students still fail to graduate on time.[6] What these statistics do not reflect are the number of transient, early dropout, and special ed. students who are not eligible for a diploma. The US ranks near the bottom of all developed countries in graduation rates (twenty-second of twenty-nine countries), and the dropout figure is alarmingly high in states such as New Mexico, where only 67.9 percent of students graduate.[7]

As educators, we know that each year there are students who do graduate from high school, but they graduate well beneath the level of achievement and engagement that could have been theirs. They go out into the world convinced that higher education, the workplace, and society may have little to offer them. They step out into the unknown wary instead of eager to meet the challenges that will be instrumental in helping them create rich and dimensional lives.

Today, there are students—learning challenged or not—moving through their elementary, middle, and high school years with little or no passion for learning, when they could be engaged and involved in,

---

6   Mark Dynarski, "Is the High School Graduation Rate Really Going Up?" Brookings, May 3, 2018, https://www.brookings.edu/research/is-the-high-school-graduation-rate-really-going-up.

7   Briana Boyington, "See High School Graduation Rates by State," US News & World Report, May 18, 2018, https://www.usnews.com/high-schools/best-high-schools/articles/2018-05-18/see-high-school-graduation-rates-by-state.

even enthralled by, the process of discovering who they are in relation to the world around them. They could be uncovering how they will fit within the world like perfectly joined pieces in the jigsaw puzzle of the universe. If they are not, we must ask ourselves, *why* not?

Isn't that what learning *should* do for everyone?

As the two of us stepped out into our own unknown, creating The Cottage School, we believed we had the answer to that question, and the answer was: Yes! Engagement *is* what education should excite in each and every child. In retrospect, we can see that the universe itself may have been leading us to that

Engagement is what education should excite in each and every child.

moment in the early 1980s, when the sum totals of our joint experiences brought us to that very revelation.

OUR ROAD TO TCS: TWO TRAINS, SAME DESTINATION

In the decade or so that preceded our founding of The Cottage School, we had, as a married couple, traveled a circuitous route through the US, Southeast Asia, Western Europe, and back again to the US.

During that time, Jacque employed her teaching certification and bachelor's in English to teach high school English to highly motivated international students in Thailand, then utilized her skills and experience to teach students in rural Shelby County, Ohio. Many of her students had previously been deemed unteachable. Jacque was recruited to teach multiple subjects to "troubled" boys at a well-known therapeutic wilderness camp in Georgia. She also earned her master's degree in behavior disorders while she held that post. Jacque then went on to serve as an educational facilitator for students with neurological and other learning challenges in the adolescent psychiatric ward at Atlanta's Peachford Hospital. Afterward, she taught life-skills and academics to severely disabled teens in a pilot program at the Sexton Woods Psychoeducational Facility, a specialized public school in DeKalb County, Georgia. There, she acquired a deep appreciation for the use of pre-vocational skills teaching, designed to provide the structure so essential in challenged learning. Jacque continued her educational journey and earned her PhD in educational administration.

When we first met at the University of Kentucky, Jacque was headed on her path as an educator, Joe as a food technologist. Joe soon found himself on the other side of the world in Vietnam, where he managed a large dairy facility for Beatrice Foods. Not long after, Joe and Jacque married in Thailand. When we returned to the states, Joe maintained his employment with Beatrice Foods and became part of the management services team operating out of Ohio. While at home, between assignments, he helped tutor students in math and science in his spare time—and found the experience more rewarding than his lucrative corporate career.

Joe has always had a head for business and he can see right through to the crux of an issue with laser-like vision. Eventually, that ability helped him see that his own mission in life was to teach. Before he could realize his dream, Joe's career in the dairy industry took us to Italy. Upon our return to the US, Joe earned his master's in science education and went on to teach science at Columbia High School in DeKalb County, Georgia. While with the county, he was transferred to Briarcliff High School and was then tapped to launch an alternative high school program for students under sixteen years old who had been expelled. It didn't take long for Joe and his team to discover that most of the expelled students were grappling with undiagnosed learning disabilities.

Joe's own path through the educational system soon landed him at The New School in the Lost Forest, an Atlanta-area independent K-12 school for students with learning disabilities. He served as upper school coordinator (principal) there until a discussion with the school's founder planted the idea of launching his own special-needs school, just as Jacque, at Sexton Woods, was coming to the same conclusion. Together, we decided it was time for us to put our combined experience and innovative approaches to work, taking two trains to the same station!

Along our journey (during a detour in Italy, in fact), we adopted our first son, Steven, and shortly thereafter, our second son, Eric, was born. By the time we initiated our two-phase plan to found a special-needs school, we were like so many other young people launching a venture: we were trying to raise a young family, pursue our own personal missions, and keep our heads above water all at the same time.

As often happens when the universe is prodding you along, at a later point we also saw our mission to transform special-needs teaching from another side entirely. We found that our older son, Steven, was struggling with his own learning challenges within the public school system. Ironically, we had committed ourselves to teaching special-needs students before we were even aware of our own child's challenges.

Yet, our personal experiences with our son's unique learning needs (and an inside look at the limitations of the public school system at the time) only strengthened our resolve to mobilize our eclectic array of unique approaches to send our students out into the world with knowledge, confidence, and independence. Steven's experience (and, later, Eric's issues with the mainstream educational system in high school) gave us additional insight—parental insight—that proved invaluable in our child-centered work.

WHAT WE BELIEVE

While the method we have developed is multi-faceted, highly dimensional, and relies on a carefully constructed "scaffold" of interdependent planks and supports, the basic tenets of the Cottage School model are not complicated at all:

- **Potential for student success.** We believe that young people impacted by their individual learning styles possess unlimited potential to uncover and express their abilities and talents. *All* students possess an unlimited potential for success in their communities, places of work, and the world at large.

- **Need for well-educated job force and citizenry.** We believe that today's rapidly accelerating world requires legions of employees with basic job-readiness skills. We believe that vibrant communities need well-educated, highly skilled, and collaborative citizens.

- **Universality of "unique" learning.** We believe that learning-challenged, neurologically challenged, and mainstream students alike have unique learning styles. Thus, we believe that *all* learners benefit greatly from a "real-life" education that is dimensional and incorporates essential life-skills in a pragmatic and highly effective manner (the TCS model).

- **Importance of life-relevant education in the twenty-first century.** We believe thoughtful, innovative, functionally modeled education (the TCS model) best ingrains the "relevance" of schooling to life *after* graduation. Importantly, it supports confidence, independence, and success in *all* facets of human life.

- **Importance of balanced and dimensional education.** We believe that all educational systems—not just those designed for students diagnosed with identified learning challenges—must expand to embrace the broad spectrum of career-based, artistic, social, and academic skills that are essential to the creation of any sustainable, productive, and richly dimensional community of citizens.

- **TCS adoption and scalability.** We believe that any caring persons—parents, educators, business and community leaders—can create a highly functional learning oasis through The Cottage School program. Programs launched on the TCS model are scalable. They can originate as an individual student's study plan (for home or blended schooling, or embedded within a more conventional program). Alternatively, they can be introduced as a local co-op or group initiative. They can even form the basis of a full-fledged community or regional school or agency.

LAUNCHING A TCS INITIATIVE FOR ONE OR ONE HUNDRED

The Cottage School evolved over three decades as it grew in program scope and facility size. Importantly, it also flourished as awareness of neurologically based learning disorders and challenges deepened, and as our students taught us more and more about themselves and their needs. That being said, the core design of the TCS program has *never* changed. We were confident we had the right recipe for success when we first began to envision the school. Results from our more than one thousand graduates, many of whom had previously found little success elsewhere, have proved we were not mistaken.

Though we have always thrived on the energy of kids who learn differently, we freely admit that we struggled with many concerns our charges never knew about, as we focused on what we cared about most—them! Those issues included

- **how to design a bona fide business plan** for our school to attract the assistance (and "guardian angels") we needed;

- **how to budget and predict cashflow** to keep our school afloat while offering the highest quality education;

- **how to find and attract the best teachers and staff** for our special kind of educational delivery;

- **how to train teachers** to "live and breathe" a new educational paradigm;

- **how to get the word out** about our venture and let parents, schools, and local professionals know our "oasis" of learning was up and running;

- **how to create a hard-working board of directors** to help lead and guide us;

- **how to partner** with professionals, schools, and agencies of benefit to our students and parents;

- **how to locate the most valuable and effective resources** for our school community;

- **how to help our parents and families augment and support** our unique approach, without our intervention in family life or structure;

- **how to attract donors and community funding and involvement** (without compromising on educational promise);

- **how to choose the best facility, property, and community** in which to house our unique school;

- **how to plan for growth** without over-expanding; and

- **how to balance our demanding school and home lives** without sacrificing our children or our mission.

While our program itself was never trial-and-error, the items above represent many of the areas that could have been pitfalls for us along the way, and today constitute a valuable portion of the TCS model road map we share with you. While we cannot share every single aspect of TCS inside these pages, we can offer you the most essential information about our model and our own journey to TCS.

Embedded in the chapters ahead, you will find everything you need for brainstorming, clarity of planning, consistency of education delivery, and—just as essential—inspiration. After reading this book, we hope you will decide, "I can do this!" and transform one life, or many, forever. Hand-in-hand with the universe, we are here for help and guidance as you make your way forward.

—Jacque and Joe Digieso, Atlanta, Georgia, 2019

CHAPTER ONE

A NEW KIND OF EDUCATION: THE COTTAGE SCHOOL

Never put a lid on a kid.

—Jacque Digieso

Everyone has a dream. Ours was all about kids and *their* dreams of succeeding in life.

We were educators, a husband and wife who had spent our careers helping children with learning challenges of all kinds, young people who struggled against mainstream education. So, we longed to create our own independent brand of schooling for students whose needs were not being met in the Atlanta, Georgia, area. We had made our home in Atlanta, and though we each had been working at a different school, we knew it was time to leave our positions (and our salaries!) and step out into the unknown. Conventional education simply was not working for legions of children who could not respond to it. These students needed an education that didn't cling to old assumptions or run along time-worn tracks. Though our concept would integrate so much of what we ourselves had learned from so many disparate teaching and life experiences, we were sure of one thing: holistically, our educational model would not be like any other we knew.

The program we envisioned would establish a new educational paradigm designed to meet the needs of students with unique learning styles—young people we knew possessed the same unlimited abilities, talents, and potential for success as their mainstream peers. Our method would employ a highly dimensional yet pragmatic approach, incorporating academic, artistic, and social skills within a framework of life-, career-, and behaviorally-based education.

The program we envisioned would establish a new educational paradigm designed to meet the needs of students with unique learning styles.

At that time, there were a smattering of schools offering education for young people with special learning needs. Yet they were largely K-8 programs, and it was clear they were mostly seeking students with average to above-average intelligence—learners who demonstrated high verbal skills but low performance skills.[8] The administrators of these schools knew they could teach such young people successfully and thus keep attracting new prospects. That left no programs designed to meet the needs of the students left behind. These were students with average to below-average intelligence who demonstrated the reverse of the "acceptable" special-needs students: their testing revealed high performance skills and low verbal skills.

---

8   As measured by IQ (or Intelligence Quotient) testing.

That meant there were no educational programs available for such adolescents who had already been disabused of the mainstream educational system.

In short, no one wanted the older kids already knocked around by the system. No one wanted the kids who refused to go to school because they couldn't bear to fail again and again and again.

BUILDING A BRIDGE TO THE COTTAGE SCHOOL

Joe was an administrator at an independent school for high-functioning, special-needs education and Jacque was utilizing pre-vocational education techniques to teach psychiatrically challenged youths at a public institution when we decided that a tutoring center would help us find out if there was a need for an individualized, structured approach to instruction in our area. We dubbed the tutoring program The Educational Resource Center and agreed that if our "test project" did reveal that need, it would also help to provide start-up funds for a special-needs school venture.

The Educational Resource Center took off and took us with it. As it happened, there was a crying need for learning support and we soon had plenty of students to instruct. Jacque, who had years of experience teaching many subjects, tutored diligently. Joe taught math and science to students in the evening. Our enrollees were soon succeeding, and parents were telling other parents about us. We even created a student transportation service for middle schoolers, to make it easier for working parents to utilize our services. Then, we added additional tutoring staff. We were growing faster than we could possibly have anticipated.

Along the way, we encountered students of all types: those who had neglected their studies and fallen behind, others who were having trouble with reading or math, kids who feared they wouldn't graduate or get into the colleges of their choice, jocks who had to pass subjects or be benched, and students with medical conditions that impacted their learning. We were receiving calls from parents of children who had been consistently struggling with schoolwork or the educational structure of their mainstream school. Many were searching for special-needs schools and hoping for help in the interim. We recognized patterns in these children, which we already knew well from our previous work, yet there were even more of these "lost" students than we had imagined: the learning-challenged, who had not been diagnosed; the kids who had been branded lazy, irresponsible, and academically unsuccessful; those who had been failed by the system at times; and those whose parents had even given up on them. Girls who came to us were often so anxiety-ridden that they had simply refused to attend school at all. Boys were acting out and getting themselves into trouble that risked suspension or worse. Eventually, we found ourselves with eight full-time students in a day tutoring program.

BATTLING A "NONEXISTENT" NEUROLOGICAL CHALLENGE

Looking back, it's hard to believe that in the early 1980s, when we were first envisioning The Cottage School, all students who experienced learning difficulties were classified only as—pick one—ADD (attention deficit disorder), dyslexic, or intellectually or learning disabled (LD). Today, the medical and psychiatric communities recognize a vast constellation of challenges that previously had been lumped together. They include attention deficit/ hyperactivity disorder (ADHD), bipolar disorder and its variations, school anxiety, ADD and its variants, autism spectrum disorder (ASD, which now incorporates Asperger's syndrome), Tourette's syndrome, numerous forms of depression, and a host of other neurological conditions such as dyslexia, dysgraphia, and obsessive compulsive disorder.

Many existing classifications are undergoing reclassification in the *DSM*. Asperger's syndrome, for instance, was rolled into the classification of ASD as recently as 2013. ASD now encompasses autistic disorder, childhood disintegrative disorder, pervasive developmental disorder-not otherwise specified (PDD-NOS), and Asperger's syndrome.

Many adolescents in our community were grappling with their learning challenges and their parents were frustrated as well. They knew their children desperately required intervention by those who truly understood their challenges, but most parents had not been able to uncover the resources for help. Many students had received a diagnosis of "intellectually disabled" while their parents were convinced that their child was of average or above-average intelligence, and grappling with significant social, developmental, or transitional issues. Some parents feared their children were self-medicating. Still, others knew that their children were dealing with non-neurological medical or physiological issues that posed insurmountable obstacles to acquiring an education in a mainstream setting. They knew their children felt like they did not fit in and were thus demoralized.

Even the parents who had been able to secure diagnoses for their children's learning challenges could not find a tactical way to help their kids make it through the area schools. There was little formal guidance available to professionals working with families or student learners. Back then, psychiatrists, psychologists, and pediatricians did not have the resources to guide families that they have today. Studies of the human brain and how information is processed have, since that time, produced data that continues to expand exponentially.[9] Today, where neurological deficits exist, unique instructional methods can be produced to create the specific structure and strategies that capitalize on an individual's strengths. At the same time, compensatory strategies can be incorporated to enable a previously struggling student to become a successful learner.

In 1984, as we envisioned our new school and its entirely new mode of education, we knew that TCS would be in the forefront of delivering such structures and strategies. That was because, through our own educational journeys, both of us had experienced firsthand the broadest variety of learners with unique needs. The Atlanta psychiatric community was also growing to meet the needs of these families, and our partnerships with those professionals allowed us to incorporate the latest neurological and psychiatric studies and findings.

The time was right. Many of the parents who began to query TCS were frantically seeking expert guidance for their struggling, high-school-aged children, our target student population. They told us that their kids were failing in school, the system was forsaking them, and they feared their children would not only continue to fall down in school, but in *life*.

---

9   We now have the *DSM V*. Diagnostic tools such as IQ testing also have been refined to paint a clearer picture of how individuals and their brains process information—a picture that includes individual strengths and weaknesses. American Psychiatric Association, *Diagnostic and Statistical Manual of Mental Disorders*, 5th ed. (Arlington, VA: American Psychiatric Publishing, 2013).

Why can't Jenny learn? The number of students in the US who struggle within the mainstream K-12 educational system is vast. The challenges those children face are frequently generated by neurological and medical conditions, but sometimes are not. In fact, there is no end to the issues that can prevent an otherwise curious and open young person from learning and succeeding in the world, for children are born with a natural need to experience the world and integrate its lessons for growth.[10] Aside from DSM- and AMA-based diagnoses, what could get in the way of that innate need? Below is a starter list of possible non-neurological issues (many of which present simultaneously), arranged alphabetically:

- anger, frustration, and anxiety (mood issues)

- boredom (not uncommon with students of above-average intelligence)

- chronic illnesses such as diabetes, epilepsy, and severe allergies

- cultural issues (level of exposure to American culture and practice, racial bias, religious practices or dress)

- family issues (dysfunction, divorce, abuse, community status, etc.)

- fear and fear of failure

---

10 In the widely respected textbook, *How People Learn: Brain, Mind, Experience, and School: Expanded Edition,* the authors look at human learning holistically, from birth onward. They point to the importance of real-life relevancy in learning, confirm that human beings have unique styles of information intake and integration, and uncover many roadblocks to learning often presented by mainstream classroom teaching.
National Research Council, *How People Learn: Brain, Mind, Experience, and School: Expanded Edition* (Washington, DC: The National Academies Press, 2000).

- food sensitivity issues that affect behavior and ability to focus
- isolation
- lack of organizational skills or self-discipline
- learning style inconsistent with teaching style
- low self-esteem
- peer pressure (bullying and hyper-competitiveness)
- physical challenges
- prescribed medication and self-medication (alcohol and drug use)
- previous negative learning experiences
- relevance (inability to see relevance of education to life)
- social issues (bullying, family and community status, and unemployment)
- trauma
- traumatic brain injury

AN EAR TO THE GROUND—AND A SHOVE

Even though we dreamed of starting our own school and had planned The Educational Resource Center as an ideal way to hold our ear to the ground to assess community need, we still needed a final nudge—or two.

The first nudge came from a local independent school when during the spring of 1984, ten tenth-grade students, mostly boys, had gotten into trouble on spring break. Rather than expel so many students, the school sent them to us for academic support. Midway through that semester of teaching the students at The Educational Resource Center, we knew we had the makings of a successful full-time program and we began to formulate plans for our special-needs high school.

The second nudge was the discussion Joe and the founder of The New School (where he was teaching at the time) had about adding life-skills to her school's curriculum. She didn't choose to adopt Joe's ideas, but suggested he launch his own school program.

So, in March 1985, The Cottage School was established—complete with a mission, ten tenets, and a clear-cut plan for a six-pillared "scaffold" that would serve as the underlayment of the TCS methodology.

In March 1985, The Cottage School was established—complete with a mission, ten tenets, and a clear-cut plan for a six-pillared "scaffold" that would serve as the underlayment of the TCS methodology.

Our Mission:

To build a sense of self for students with special learning needs, through academic and experiential programming, The Cottage School prepares students for fulfillment of their true potential as confident, productive, and independent adults.

Our Ten Tenets:

1. Every student can **succeed** at something.

2. Focus on **strengths** to build the individual.

3. **Safety** enables risk-taking, which leads to growth.

4. Create a **future of possibilities.**

5. **Show up!** Nothing good can happen if you don't show up prepared.

6. **Be present!** (Not being present and paying attention says: "You don't matter.")

7. **Policies** are consistent, but flexible.

8. **Role models** are powerful individuals.

9. **Connecting** to others builds relationships.

10. **Communication** connects us.

THE SIX PILLARS OF THE COTTAGE SCHOOL (TCS) SCAFFOLD

The special-needs schools in the greater Atlanta and surrounding area all had one thing in common at that time: they provided programming for students whose IQ tests revealed average to above-average intelligence, learners who demonstrated high verbal skills with low performance skills. But there were no programs designed to meet the needs of students who were hands-on learners, whose testing revealed average intelligence and a combination that was the reverse of the students other schools were accepting: high performance skills with lower or commensurate verbal skills.

IQ testing was then, and still is, the jumping-off point for most learning-potential assessments. Its two components (assessing verbal skills and performance skills) also comprise sub-tests which reveal very specific strengths and weaknesses. To us, this secondary information was all-important. It pointed to students' undeveloped or underdeveloped potential (strengths) and the issues (weaknesses) that were merely roadblocks, not predictors of failure.

These were the kids who demonstrated the greatest potential for dropping out of high school, engaging in antisocial activities, and turning to self-medication to numb themselves to the roadblocks in their lives. They were the students that we targeted for The Cottage School. They were high school-aged kids we knew had innate and valuable talents and skills that could be developed. Helping them develop their skills would empower them to move confidently into the world beyond high school and especially the workplace. We knew we could create a highly specific yet individualized learning structure or "scaffold" that would help us add these previously lost young people to the world of happy, productive, and contributing adults.

> **We knew we could create a highly specific yet individualized learning structure or "scaffold" that would help us add these previously lost young people to the world of happy, productive, and contributing adults.**

Like any scaffold, the structure we envisioned would depend on a series of supporting uprights (standards or pillars) positioned on a solid base plate to distribute the weight they support. The key support components of our scaffold encompassed the following tenants.

One: A Culture of Safety

Simply put, The Cottage School would be constructed around a culture where students felt *safe*.

We knew that too many special-needs students had spent years inside mainstream education where they could not trust others to accept them or offer them the same opportunities afforded to their classmates; where teachers and fellow students did not try to understand or work with them, assist them, show them patience, listen to their issues, or treat them as they treated "typical" peers.

We recognized that, above all else, The Cottage School must be a place where our students felt safe to trust anyone in the TCS community, without exception. Our students must feel safe to speak about anything, say what they need to say, and disagree with others about anything as long as they did so in a civil manner.

Our students would be able to fail without reprisal. They would be free to make mistakes without being humiliated, ostracized, or punished. On the contrary, they would be encouraged to risk mistakes for the sake of progress, growth, and innovation.

Our students—and the TCS structure itself—could not be placed at risk by behavior that could undermine the safety of the school culture. We would therefore rely on students and parents alike to abide by an agreement that identified Thirteen Behaviors of Concern.[11] These behaviors would immediately trigger response and remedy to ensure the protection of all within the TCS community and to support the success of the student in question. (More about the Thirteen Behaviors of Concern in chapters 5 and 10.)

Importantly, our students had to feel safe to be who they are, so that we could assess and develop the *real child and their special learning needs. That meant self-medicating in any manner (widespread at the time) could not be permitted.*[12] We would require students and families to formally agree to the testing as a condition of enrollment and also as a "for cause" response (included in the Thirteen Behaviors

---

11 Among other items, The Thirteen Behaviors of Concern include abrupt changes in attitude, sudden or continuing decline in attendance at school, declining level of performance, stealing, and possession of drugs, alcohol, or drug paraphernalia. See chapter 10 for the additional behaviors listed.

12 The Cottage School was the first independent school in the region to institute "For Cause" drug testing.

of Concern). There would be no finger-pointing, no judgment. The drug-testing program would exist only to identify an issue that needed to be remedied to ensure a student's success.[13]

Finally, we understood that, absent an environment in which students were safe to thrive, no other pillar of our TCS scaffold would be able to stand, let alone support additional segments of the TCS structure.

Two: Educational Balance—Individualized Learning

The TCS education must represent a balance of the many components that support human growth mentally, physically, and otherwise. Our students, each with unlimited potential, would find their skills and talents in academics, the arts, sports, technology, business, and a constellation of interest areas. Our educational program would evolve to open doors in all directions while providing a student-driven study plan that was individualized for each unique learner.

Increasingly, mainstream education was being reconfigured to meet broad, state-funded, and other dictates focused on one-size-fits-all academic testing. More and more, mainstream education was de-emphasizing the arts, sports, electives, and other holistic endeavors. A TCS education would be balanced, and yet, individualized, to ensure development of the mind, soul, and human spirit, which we knew to be as interdependent as the scaffold we sought to create. Our graduates would venture into the world with a solid academic base and a portfolio of unique skills and talents that their TCS education had uncovered, identified, and nurtured. We envisioned the TCS

---

13 The drug-testing program, dubbed "For Cause," was developed in cooperation with the child and adolescent psychiatrist, Dr. Dirk E. Huttenbach of Smyrna, Georgia. We later traveled around the country with Dr. Huttenbach, demonstrating how the drug testing, triggered by one of the Behaviors of Concern, would prevent the masking of neurological, medical, and developmental issues.

scaffold as one so well constructed that certain supports *could (and would) be removed, à la Jenga,*[14] as a student became stronger and better able to succeed on his or her own.

Three: Accountability and Awareness of Cause and Effect

From the start, both of us knew that instilling a solid sense of accountability plus the awareness of cause and effect would be central to the TCS program—as it should be to *any* educational program. To send a young person out into adult life with no real understanding of accountability and consequences is to impede upon all attempted progress. On the other hand, to fully equip a student with those skills is to give a direct route to successful endeavors.

To ensure our students would grasp, internalize, and readily call up these skills, we developed a continual feedback system that would make it impossible for any TCS student not to "see" how he or she was doing. The mock-pay system we developed is based on each student's achievement of specific goals in our TCS "workplace"—just as pay (along with recognition, reward, self-satisfaction, and personal and career progress) is a measure of how well we do or don't do our jobs in real life.

With our Pay Level system,[15] each student would receive a Cottage School checkbook. An hourly wage for work completed and participation would be credited to each student's account. The "pay"

---

14   In the game of Jenga, players take turns removing one block at a time from a tower constructed of fifty-four blocks. Ironically, since the game is all about removing supports from a structure, the name Jenga is derived from *kujenga,* a Swahili word which means "to build."

15   The TCS Pay Level system is a proprietary system developed by the Digiesos. It is a multidimensional, intricate behavior modification system designed to recognize students' increasing levels of responsibility and internalization of the TCS program structure. The process, originally organized across five levels for high school students, is also customized for middle and elementary school students.

could be used to purchase leisure or personal-interest activities, such as extra-curricular sports or off-campus trips.

The identical pay goals would be in place for all students and, each class hour, a student's compensation would be based on the achievement of clear and universal goals (see upcoming box, "Job Ready and Life Ready"). Payment would also be based on a consistent, predictable, and reliable basis (no surprises) and would be non-judgmental (the clearly communicated cause and effect would ensure objectivity). That is, a student would either complete a task or not. Skills demonstrated would receive compensation; skills not demonstrated would result in less than full pay. For example, payment would be reduced for non-completion of homework. Consequently, diminished pay might require that a student purchase academic assistance instead of paying to participate in a much-anticipated bowling event.

We designed our Pay Level system to ensure that it was difficult for a student *not* to receive some pay for each class period. And, importantly, each student would receive immediate feedback regarding the skills and behavior that were achieved and those that needed strengthening. Just as workers learn in real life, our Pay Level system would send the message that in the real world, people pay for the work completed, not for services not rendered or products not delivered.

Just as workers learn in real life, our Pay Level system would send the message that in the real world, people pay for the work completed, not for services not rendered or products not delivered.

Our students would learn to manage life, not allow it to buffet them about. They would quickly grasp that it was entirely up to them to be on time, complete their work, and dress appropriately for their situations. We were confident that, working within our mock-pay system as in life, our students' successes would breed even greater success.

Four: Focus on Transition

We knew that the ability to progress comfortably through transitions was not just a challenge for the students we targeted at The Cottage School—in fact, transitioning is difficult for many students. Parents often wonder why their child has such difficulty making it from bed to breakfast table to car to school. Even veteran teachers rail against such eternal student behaviors as being late for school, late for class, late with assignments, and a failure to study.

Yet the truth is, there are plenty of us who cannot easily process very specific sets of expectations. Entrepreneurs and top executives such as Virgin CEO Richard Branson and Turner Broadcasting's Ted Turner confide that they sought alternative career situations and daily workarounds because of their learning challenges.[16] What turns out to have been ADD, ADHD, Asperger's syndrome, and other neurological challenges may have caused countless business leaders to struggle to get to the office on time, make it across town for meetings, or even attend business dinners and events. Ironically, experts now theorize that a prevalence of neurologically based learning disorders in recent generations may actually be responsible for the bumper crops of innovative, out-of-the-box thinkers behind many of our twenty-first-century advances.[17] (This only confirms our convictions about the deep wells of untapped potential in unique learners.) Indi-

---

16   Dylan Love, "15 CEOs with Learning Disabilities," Business Insider, May 2011, https://www.businessinsider.com/ceo-learning-disabilities-2011-5.

17   David Cox, "A Learning Disability Often Makes for a More Visionary, Innovative CEO," Quartz, May 2015, https://qz.com/413783/learning-disability-makes-for-a-more-visionary-innovative-ceo/.

viduals like Branson and Turner forced themselves to find ways to ingeniously manage their transitional difficulties. Most who wrestle with transitioning, however, can certainly use qualified assistance.

To many adults, transitioning is the way of life. But to a developing young person—especially one who faces significant challenges with change of all kinds—transitioning can seem abstract and excruciating. In our educational journeys, we had firsthand experience with the power of transitioning difficulty to derail learning. We knew we needed to create a *concrete* set of behaviors that would serve as a vehicle to painlessly and mechanically transport a student from one situation to another.

To many adults, transitioning is the way of life. But to a developing young person—especially one who faces significant challenges with change of all kinds—transitioning can seem abstract and excruciating.

That set of behaviors formed the base of the TCS scaffold. It established a true working environment, in which each student would be treated as an "employee" of TCS. Students would, for example, clock-in to school each morning via a physical act which enabled them to shift gears and prepare for the challenges at hand. Rooted in applied behavioral analysis, the simple act of inserting a punch card in a time clock[18] signals that the workday has begun.

JOB READY AND LIFE READY

Corporate leaders have confided to us that they see a sizable gap between what is currently being taught in mainstream schools and what they are

---

18   These days, a modern fingerprint scan has taken the place of that timeclock at The Cottage School.

looking for in employees. They tell us that they wish their employees had learned the life- and work-skills that TCS students so enthusiastically demonstrate. Those skills ensure that our students' future employers will hire engaged, contributing workers who can help their companies offer better products, services, and innovations across the globe. Business people who interact with TCS students maintain that TCS is an educational model for *all* learners.

Yet it is our TCS students who are the direct beneficiaries of their job- and life-ready education. For, after TCS kids taste success, they blossom into students, and then leaders. They graduate with the knowledge that their success knows few limits.

Today, the press coverage of millennials and Gen-Zers in the marketplace (many of whom live at home well into their thirties[19]) makes it clear that even mainstream high school and college graduates venture out into the world wobbly about life and with trepidation about the world of work.[20] Common fears are: How do I apply and interview for a job? What will be expected of me at work? How will I fit in? How do I find a place to live? How will I manage salary, bills, and higher-education debts by myself?

TCS graduates know few, if any, of these fears because they have been educated in the TCS workplace, which teaches not just academics, the

---

19 Richard Fry, "It's Becoming More Common for Young Adults to Live at Home—and for Longer Stretches," Pew Research Center, May 5, 2017, http://www.pewresearch.org/fact-tank/2017/05/05/its-becoming-more-common-for-young-adults-to-live-at-home-and-for-longer-stretches.

20 Libby Page, "How to Deal with Employability Anxiety," The Guardian, May 19, 2014, https://www.theguardian.com/education/2014/may/19/employment-anxiety-students-job-worry.

arts, music, and sports, but also the skills needed for confidently navigating real life and the world of work.

The following **five job-readiness or life-skills** are essential to the TCS model:

1. Punctuality

2. Being prepared for the task at hand

3. Communicating in an appropriate manner

4. Dressing appropriately

5. Completing tasks at hand

These five behaviors are used as a basis for the Pay Level incentive. Many other areas of job readiness are also core to the TCS program and are necessary for future success. They include the ability to

- advocate for oneself;

- manage time, tasks, and goal achievement;

- present oneself effectively; and

- be aware of and control facial expressions and body language.

How many of today's young hires can ace all of these job-readiness skills? TCS graduates can.

Five: Focus on Organization

It is no surprise to parents and teachers that organization can present a very real challenge to any student. (Neurologically, this is referred to as executive functioning.) We knew that, diagnosed or not, an inability to organize effectively would be even more challenging for the TCS student. The mainstream educational system assumes—not always correctly—that students will intuitively pick up the organizational capabilities so essential to the learning process and a productive adult life. We left nothing to intuition. Threaded throughout the TCS scaffold would be the kind of organization support and behavioral training generally absent in mainstream schooling.

In the TCS program, homeroom, for instance, would serve as much more than the congregation point it represents in conventional high schools. Under the guidance of the carefully trained homeroom teacher, TCS students practice the skills involved in preparing and organizing their work and thoughts for the day's activities ahead. They also conscientiously prepare for the work and study to be completed at home in the evening. In homeroom, organizational practices become ingrained in the same way they are designed to throughout the TCS program: through concerted, strategic program planning and repetitive reinforcement.

Six: Focus on Tracking

Though it sounds elementary, keeping track of what we have to do in life is a skill that eludes many adults, and trips up all of us at times. Even the tasks that are most important to us can slip through our fingers when we lose track of them. What parent has not exclaimed at some point, "I forgot to pick up the kids! They're waiting at school!" or "I can't believe I missed my favorite aunt's birthday!" Adults with fairly well-developed life-skills can rebound from such lapses and quickly construct remedies. Younger people, however, can be at a loss to correct such situations. Students with special needs can be so overwhelmed by tasks dropped or mounting that more serious reactions ensue.

We knew it was necessary to create a system that could be used by all students, regardless of ability, to keep track of assignments.

Understanding expectations and tracking what has been completed and what still needs to be done was essential to weave into our students' daily structure. Parents of special-needs students, especially, too often hear that their child received a failing grade on an assignment because she "forgot" there *was* an assignment. A teacher's protest, "Well, I told the class—" means little when parents know that their child has trouble retaining verbally delivered assignment information. Auditory processing—the ability to hear a set of directions and successfully store them in long-term memory—is not a skill everyone possesses. Even directions written on the classroom board can go astray when a student neglects to jot them down or can't recall where they were scribbled.

A teacher's protest, "Well, I told the class—" means little when parents know that their child has trouble retaining verbally delivered assignment information.

Once again, a universal tracking system was our answer. A two-week "planner" was designed specifically to record assignments for each class period time-block across the two school weeks. A space for the teacher's signature was included to ensure a student's pay for recording an assignment and completing it. No student would be singled out to use a planning helper. All students would utilize the identical organizational method.

A PRESCRIPTIVE PLAN

We were unafraid to develop a plan that was prescriptive. Data provided in each student's psychological/educational testing would allow the faculty to design an educational approach based on the identified strengths while addressing the diagnosed weaknesses. Our students would be able to rely on the universality of the TCS environment: what went for one, went for all. They would feel safe in a school where no one was singled out as different or above the rules. No one would be prey to mistreatment. The consistency of the educational message would offer the type of security all humans feel in knowing that the sun will rise each day and set each evening.

Five Takeaways

1. Every student has areas of strength; those strengths need only to be uncovered, identified, and nurtured.

2. All students desire to be successful; a student's environment either fans that desire like a flame or extinguishes it by drowning it or allowing embers to go cold through neglect.

3. Providing an educational structure or "scaffold" builds on strengths and results in success.

4. Teaching compensatory strategies empowers students and builds self-esteem. (Entrepreneurs and innovators learn to "compensate" and their achievements soar because they must innovate!)

5. Prescriptive educational plans equals successful learners.

CHAPTER TWO

THE HUB OF TCS: TEACHER TRAINING

Ninety-nine percent of all employees want to do a good job. How they perform is simply a reflection of the one for whom they work.

—**Mark S. Hoplamazian, president of Hyatt Hotels**[21]

It was the first morning session of our one-week pre-planning Teacher Training Session. Matt, one of our new hires, looked uncomfortable. As we and our teacher trainers discussed the carefully "modified milieu" in which our TCS teachers would be working, we noted that Matt squirmed in his seat and grew paler by the minute. We were concerned: at one point, he looked as though he might pass out. The lunch break finally came and Matt made for the door ahead of his fellow hirelings. When our new teachers returned for the afternoon of training, we noticed that Matt did not. Later, we heard that he had confided training was "way more than I thought it would be." Clearly,

---

21 Linda M. Orr and Dave J. Orr, *Eliminating Waste in Business: Run Lean, Boost Profitability* (New York City: Apress Books, 2014).

teaching within the TCS-modified milieu is not for everyone—nor should it be.

NO ONE WANTS TO FAIL

If the quotation heading this chapter strikes you as solely about those in business, think again: *everyone* wants to do a good job in work, in school, in life. No one sets out to fail, yet the environment in which we work, study, and operate on a daily basis can support us or thwart us at every turn. We knew the situation would be no different in our school. Our faculty and staff must be comprised of those who were determined to succeed for our kids. Their success was critical to the success of our students.

Most real-life employees will tell you it is specifically the individual for whom they work who has the greatest impact on their ability to produce and succeed. Thus, interactions between our "employees" (students) and their "bosses" (teachers) had to support and nurture progress. Those interactions could do irreparable harm if the educators we put in place to teach and guide them were not 100 percent aligned with the TCS model.

Hiring and training, then, had to ensure uniformity of mission, action, and culture throughout the faculty. With our charges already battle-fatigued (and in some cases, traumatized) from their experiences inside a mainstream educational system not designed to accommodate them, there was little room for error. A single teacher reproof, "How could you be so stupid?" or well-intentioned detour, "I'll sign off on your pay even though your homework is incomplete," could effectively steer our program right off its rails.

THE NEUROLOGY BEHIND LEARNING DIFFERENCES

As children, we arrive in this world externally motivated for the most part. We want food and shelter and we want to be comfortable. Yet for all that we need, we're dependent on everything outside of ourselves. The process of maturing is all about taking that external motivation and making it internal, intrinsic motivation. Most teenagers still assume that everything is "outside" them, beyond their control. It is a crucial process for any parent or educator to help adolescents *internalize* that motivation before they step out into the world and try to make a living themselves. For our TCS kids, specifically ADHD kids, this would be even more critical, as they have difficulty understanding why things happen in general, and how they're connected.

We saw that the TCS teacher-student relationship, initially, would be very external. At first, earning an hourly pay is a huge motivator. However, the relationship between a TCS student and teacher relies on the student's need to believe that the teacher has his best interest at heart—something that child may not have experienced in a long time. Previously, his teachers may not have rewarded or valued him, and were not necessarily interested in promoting what was best for him. But the TCS teacher is different and the student has no reason to *not* want to please that teacher by doing well. This concept of wanting to please the person that you're "working" for is exactly how learning begins. Then, as the student becomes a more

The relationship between a TCS student and teacher relies on the student's need to believe that the teacher has his best interest at heart—something that child may not have experienced in a long time.

mature learner, he is no longer learning and succeeding for his mentor. He is doing it for himself.

In finding and training the best possible teachers for our Cottage School students, our goal was to move students from an external focus to an internal one.

FINDING AND DEVELOPING THE IDEAL TCS TEACHER

Though it may sound counterintuitive, the first thing we decided was that we did not want to hire high school teachers based primarily on their experience with special-needs students. What we were seeking were instructors with deep expertise in their subject-matter areas—certified in math, science, social studies, and language arts. That decision has proven to be the right one: our students, previously considered incapable of pursuing subjects such as algebra, chemistry, or a foreign language, have successfully completed trigonometry, physics, and fourth-year Spanish or French.

We wanted to not only prepare our students academically, but also introduce them to potential career opportunities and interests they may otherwise never have discovered. Initially, the non-academic portions of our program were largely taught by TCS "consultants." As our faculty grew, these classes became part of their afternoon responsibilities. Today, our experiential classes are primarily taught by our teaching force with talents to share. Our academic staff often serves in dual roles (for instance, the math wizard whose other love is drama). Academic teachers at The Cottage School are often eager to share their knowledge and skill in experiential classes outside of their primary focus. Because of the instinctual nature of their instruction, these educators bring passion to their classes and introduce our students to the richness of life. Learning becomes irresistible. Activities such as horticulture, mountain biking, culinary arts, drama, chorus, swimming, and horseback riding, for example, are an important part of the TCS curriculum.

With instructors of all types well equipped in their disciplines, we were confident in our driving conviction: that our students would be able perform at grade level or even above. We wanted to smash the stereotype that learning-challenged kids could not handle high school material. But we knew that as long as unique learners were taught by special ed teachers whose focus was not on subject content, that stereotype was going to persist. Conversely, we understood that a student—any student—who falls in love with science, art, or drama, for instance, does so because of an inspirational teacher.

> **We wanted to smash the stereotype that learning-challenged kids could not handle high school material.**

Beyond true subject matter proficiency, we were seeking teachers we believed would be receptive to our TCS philosophy. We sought teachers willing to learn about neurological, developmental, and other learning challenges still unclassified. We also looked for those individuals who possessed a dedicated constitution (strong enough not to waver from the prescriptive TCS structure) and mindful temperament that would be best-suited to our program. We knew that many, if not most, of our teachers would have been exposed to students with neurological deficits. But back in the mid-1980s, a teacher may not have recognized a particular condition, either because it had not yet been identified, or because that individual was not trained to recognize the deficit. In today's world, virtually every teacher has encountered ADHD, bipolar disorder, depression, and dysgraphia.[22] Teachers had then, too; they just didn't always know what it was or what to do about it.

Often, though they may not have realized it, many teachers who applied to us were already prejudiced against students with unique learning issues because, in their mainstream experiences, such students didn't "fit the mold." In 1985 (and even a decade later), we knew we might have to unteach and then rewire a certain number of habits and attitudes. We hoped to limit that counterproductive process where we could. So, especially in the beginning, we preferred to work with recent teaching graduates who were more or less blank slates. Then, as now, for our high schoolers, we looked first for those experienced in their subject area, not those pre-trained in special needs with years of preset notions to dispel—usually a futile undertaking in any event. For our elementary and middle school faculty, where we placed such a heavy emphasis on the early *learning* process, we sought teachers with special-needs backgrounds, notably specialists well-versed in reading issues.

We also looked for teachers who would shake up gender expectations. At The Cottage School, we've hired female instructors who teach carpentry, auto mechanics, and shop, and male teachers who share their skills in domestic science (home economics), and dance. From the start, it was imperative we demonstrate to our students that in the real world, anyone can do anything.

Not surprisingly, TCS faculty wear a lot of hats: they're senior club and yearbook sponsors, and the like. Almost every teacher is in charge of some other activity or club. TCS teachers model for their students that human beings possess diverse skills, talents, and

---

22 Dysgraphia is a learning disability that affects writing abilities and can present as difficulties putting thoughts on paper, spelling or handwriting issues, or other manifestations. (American Psychiatric Association, op. cit.)

interests. The breadth of their presence throughout the TCS program also provides an added benefit for TCS kids, as teachers experience the students from many vantage points. We can't overemphasize the value of an instructor seeing a student come to life in sports or robotics when the same instructor knew that student only as one confounded by algebra or terrified of speaking in public.

We can't overemphasize the value of an instructor seeing a student come to life in sports or robotics when the same instructor knew that student only as one confounded by algebra or terrified of speaking in public.

More than anything else, we wanted teachers who loved teaching. Our goal was to empower our students to discover their own interests and become passionate about them. That only happens through access to the best possible teachers. Before long, the word got out that The Cottage School was a place for teachers who loved doing what they do best, not a bastion of educational bureaucracy. Soon, we didn't have to search for teachers. They found us.

It's important to note here that both TCS faculty *and* staff are hired, onboarded, and trained in the same manner. Anyone who works at The Cottage School undergoes intensive neurology and special learning training and acquires the same knowledge as everyone else. That's because, from the start, we thought: How would we be able to control the culture of safety within The Cottage School by any other means? We shuddered at the vision of a TCS student encountering an office administrator, for example, who unthinkingly chastised, or else enabled, non-TCS behavior. We wanted to make sure that *everyone* on campus—teachers, students, and staff alike— would inhabit a role that makes a difference somehow, somewhere.

FOR LOVE OF MATH: A TEACHER MAKES A DIFFERENCE

Last year, Jonathan Haines[23] spoke to TCS seniors at their annual luncheon and talked about the lost boy he once was. He had come to us in the late 1990s from a mainstream middle school—a small, shy, invisible kid with ADHD and probably other issues that were tough to diagnose at the time. Jonathan struggled with math and had been told, for as long as he could recall, that he was useless at it. He couldn't effectively add, subtract, multiply, or divide; yet testing revealed math-reasoning scores that were outstanding.

Then, at TCS, Jonathan's math teacher, Ryan, saw something in his student no one else had before. Ryan was a graduate of Georgia Tech who *lived* math, and he knew another math mind when he saw one. Teacher and student bonded and when Jonathan graduated, it was with remarkable math capability and accomplishment.

Johnathan went on to college and then became a math teacher, too. He went on to become a department head and got his master's degree. Now he is working on his PhD while he heads the math program for the county where he lives. Jonathan loves his life in mathematics because, years ago, a TCS teacher who also loved math helped him find his way.

---

23 Names are changed throughout to protect privacy.

TCS TRAINING

The ongoing professional training program that we created between 1984–85 was then, and continues to be, unique. The TCS teacher handbook we put together at that time—still our teaching "bible"— represents proprietary professional development aggregated from diverse sources, including from our own years of experience teaching special-needs students. Importantly, essential segments of ongoing TCS training come directly from psychologists, psychiatrists, speech pathologists, and other education professionals. To ensure relevancy, this handbook is reviewed annually by faculty and staff. Revisions are made as appropriate. For the last two years, TCS teachers have been recognized at the annual Georgia Independent School Association Conference as outstanding Teachers of the Year.

Even in the early years, when our budget was lean, we sent our teachers to seminars, conferences, and every learning opportunity possible by seeking donations for their ongoing professional development. After a time, when it became apparent to the educational, professional, and regional communities that The Cottage School was doing something extraordinary, we urged our teachers to present at such events, spreading the word and attracting even more outstanding teachers.

The neurological training at The Cottage School is focused on cognitive behavioral therapy and behavioral modification systems (applied behavioral analysis). Faculty and staff are intensively trained to be non-judgmental and not to personalize or escalate a student's withdrawn, hostile, or confounding behavior. Instead, teachers learn to provide students with acceptable alternative behaviors, or to defuse an intense situation with natural consequences. TCS faculty are trained to refrain from resorting to punishment reprisal. Behavior management is a critical component of maintaining a safe environment—one of the cornerstones of the TCS structure.

Neurological training is ongoing. New teacher training in neurology is embedded throughout the week. Every new faculty member has a mentor teacher to help assist in the challenging educational process. Professional development is a separate entity.

New teacher training in neurology is embedded throughout the week. Every new faculty member has a mentor teacher to help assist in the challenging educational process.

On Mondays and Thursdays we conduct teacher development sessions, with Monday sessions focused on sharing. Each teacher is encouraged to bring up cognitive and behavioral issues that others may have encountered, and for which they may be able to offer strategies and solutions or at least support and understanding. Thursday sessions are more organizational.

The collaborative sessions are hard work, and newbies sometimes protest that they've got papers to grade and things to do, with no time to "sit around and talk" or engage in the faculty "fun" activities (volleyball, bowline, etc.) designed to reduce stress and facilitate bonding. By year's end, though, the new teacher "gets it" and everything gels. "If only I had known how transformative this type of collaboration would be!" is the type of comment we often hear from our new hires at the end of their first school year. Certainly, our teachers need to collaborate, but they also need to laugh and play together, or TCS wouldn't work.

PARTNERING FOR DIMENSIONAL TRAINING

Over the years, the training budget as a whole has grown exponentially, but in the beginning, many of our professional training partners provided presentation services to us, gratis. Frankly, it was good marketing for them, because referrals worked in both directions: they needed to be able to direct their client families to the best schools for unique learners, and we needed to be able to help our student families with professional assistance when it was needed. Importantly, the more our teachers understood about their students' neurological and behavioral issues, the more accurately they could interact with families.

Importantly, our partner-experts were able to provide an in-depth understanding of the various testing data used to determine specific strengths and weaknesses. They also contributed to the development of prescriptive lesson plans that would better enable teachers to impart knowledge and helped train teachers to evaluate the knowledge that students demonstrated. Additionally, our training partners introduced strategies to help us assist students in their efforts to learn. (The "rehearsal" technique, for instance, allows students fearful of being randomly called on to participate in class.)

Professionals have routinely trained TCS teachers and staff on issues that affect students, such as Tourette's syndrome, dyslexia, and ADHD. Though we were capable of addressing those subjects ourselves, being able to host experts such as Sheryl Pruitt[24]—who can speak specifically to Tourette's syndrome, share compelling experi-

---

24   Sheryl Pruitt MEd, ET/P, is the clinical director of Parkaire Consultants, Marietta, Georgia, founded to serve neurologically impaired individuals.
Sheryl K. Pruitt, Marilyn P. Dorbush, *Teaching the Tiger: A Handbook for Individuals Involved in the Education of Students with Attention Deficit Disorders, Tourette Syndrome or Obsessive-Compulsive Disorder* (Marietta, GA: Hope PR/Parkaire Press, 1995).

ences, and explain the most current neurology—is powerful. Having presenters come to us from the Marcus Center for Autism[25] and illuminate the spectrum of that condition for our educators, has been invaluable. Not long ago, we conducted an entire year of professional development led by two internationally renowned specialists from the Emory Clinic,[26] who helped us deliver exceptional education to our new teachers and reinforce the science of applied behavior management for our more veteran faculty. We've even hosted experts in mindfulness and reflexology to help our faculty better understand the importance of relaxation both for their students and themselves.

As students grow in self-esteem and confidence, family dynamics change as well. It is not uncommon for a parent to ask us, "What have you done to my child?" and then remark, "He helps set the table for dinner and is now straightening his room without being asked. He is so intent on being on time for school that he's revamping our whole family's morning schedule!"

To assist parents with the changes occurring, and to offer in-depth education on learning neurology and other topics, The Cottage School provides meetings with professional speakers, psychiatrists, psychologists, education professionals, and other experts. We also inform our parents of upcoming educational conferences on relative topics.

Many business members who present at TCS represent the community at large—a community with vital interests in the contributions our students will be making to the regional workforce.

We have always partnered with experts in the business sector, some of whom are the parents of our students. Many business members who present

---

25   Atlanta, Georgia

26   Atlanta, Georgia

at TCS represent the community at large—a community with vital interests in the contributions our students will be making to the regional workforce. These business leaders discuss the importance of knowing how to communicate in the workplace, how to dress, why technology is so important, and how to behave in a business setting. They conduct mock interviews that carry a great deal of weight for our young people. During both Career Days and within our Career Café setting (a lunch-with-the-business community program origi-nally for high schoolers, but later on for middle schoolers as well), our business speakers continually draw audiences beyond capacity. These business partners open up a world of possibilities to excite the imaginations and ambitions of our students.

The Cottage School has been trend setting in many aspects, but notably in that it approaches career exploration with depth and breadth, and early in the game. These career-focused opportunities are not designed to coincide with the college application process (which, frankly, comes too late for real benefit), but to enhance TCS life and experiential learning from every angle. Career exploration is key to our curriculum across the board.

A TRULY INDIVIDUALIZED IEP

While an Individual Education Plan (IEP) is mandated by the federal government for all qualified special-education students in the public schools, TCS provides an IEP for *all* enrolled students. At TCS, identified staff lead the IEP training process as mentors; when the teachers understand and can integrate the process, they handle it on their own. The homeroom teachers (responsible for each student's IEP) send out forms to parents prior to IEP discussions, so that parents and students can discuss goals ahead of time. They also advise throughout the IEP process. The objective is to elicit from both parent and student what each considers to be the student's strengths, areas of needed assistance, and goals.

ESSENTIALS OF THE IEP

In many educational settings, the student's Individualized Education Plan (IEP) is developed by the school's educational team, in the absence of the student. Not so at TCS, where the process is *managed* (not determined) by TCS educators. Here are the general steps.

1. **The process launches as a family survey sent home**, prompting the parents to share valuable observations about the student to be considered during the IEP planning discussions.

2. **The student also completes a survey**, outlining his or her own general academic, social-emotional, and post-secondary goals for that school year.

3. **The faculty members complete surveys** for each student, and for each class in which the student is enrolled, incorporating data from the student's psychological/educational testing.

4. **All surveys are submitted to the process coordinator** at least one week prior to conducting the IEP.

5. **With all documents in hand, IEP construction begins.** The student, the student's parents, the homeroom teacher, and the school counselor meet to begin devising the student's IEP, primarily utilizing the student's feedback sheet and focusing on at least one existing area

of strength to begin with. Areas of growth important to the parents are also discussed.

6. **The student is consulted regarding non-school-related areas of concern** he or she would like to work on.

7. **Specific (observable and measurable) academic IEP goals are set for each subject.**

8. **The student sets the social-emotional goals for the year**, based on the student's review of the social-emotional portion of the survey and the psychological/educational battery.

9. **The student discusses plans for after graduation based on the post-secondary portion** of the survey. Post-secondary goals are set, including course direction that the school ensures is attainable.

10. **The student's goals for the year, dictated by the student, are documented**, distributed to parents and teaching staff, and attached to the student's planner.

Just as setting a budget is essential to planning expenditures to make certain hard-earned funds aren't wasted or misdirected, setting goals for a life and career is essential. The Individualized Educational Plan is essential for every TCS student. In effect, the IEP creates the benchmark for the year. It then systematically identifies the steps necessary to reach those goals—something many adults may never have plotted in their lives.

Most importantly, the TCS IEP is student-centered. It is the *student* who creates her plan, carries it with her each day, and uses it as a guide; the TCS IEP is not simply a filed document in the counselor's office. Unlike so many of the documents that are created for students during their school years, the TCS IEP is accessible for all. Because the IEP is an intentional plan, the teacher must be exceedingly careful when leading the planning process. Goals should be attainable, yet significant. Including a goal to reduce the amount of extraneous talking a student does in science class, for instance, may be an excellent one, for it may augment the student's very potential to succeed in that discipline. IEP goals may be academic, neurological, behavioral, and even personal. Goals should be very specific, observable, and measurable: "This semester I am going to achieve an eighty-eight or higher in algebra," or "This year, I will make three new friends."

Students, teachers, and parents set a goal for the post-secondary plan. While a ninth-grader's goals are developed to identify strengths and weaknesses ("What do I think I'm good at?"), a senior's post-secondary plan might specify, "I'm going to apply to three technical schools."

When it comes to teaching in conjunction with the IEP, the key is to help the student learn to manage his *own* IEP, not manage it for him by detailing assignments for every hour of every school day. The idea is to create a structure wherein the student can break down his goals into realistic segments and stay on track. The teacher's job is to walk the student through those skills, not assume those skills will be mysteriously acquired.

TCS graduates, in their life-skills-focused curriculum, learn either to internalize time- and project-management skills or adopt time-management systems.

In the business world, breaking down goals into achievable segments plotted over time is called "chunking." Today, employers find that incoming generations of young people are curiously lacking in such time- and project-management skills. Many of today's young people graduate with little knowledge of planning, quality control, and due diligence—all of which are essential in the business world. But TCS graduates, in their life-skills-focused curriculum, learn either to internalize time- and project-management skills or adopt time-management systems. No wonder regional employers like to hire TCS grads!

TWELVE FUNDAMENTALS OF TCS TEACHER TRAINING

Undergirding the structure of the many teacher training issues discussed in this chapter are a dozen fundamentals that are persistently reinforced at every possible opportunity, to ensure we are consistently building buy-in. TCS teachers must not only understand, but must internalize the following:

1. **Every student has one or more strengths.** Find those strengths, celebrate them, and build on them.

2. **Students must feel safe to rise to the challenges of the classroom.** Safety is a function of a consistent, reliable, and dependable environment.

3. **Students work first to please their teacher. Develop a rapport with your students.** Sit with the student body during break and lunch. Always model professional standards.

4. **By your presence, you will catch students doing something right.** Supervision matters!

5. **Teachers consistently reinforce expectations** every class throughout the day, each and every

day. (With universal expectations, it's easy to spot weak links.)

6. **Real behavioral change is the result of consistency over time.** Be constant. Be persistent. No teacher or parent enabling!

7. **You are powerful individuals. How are you using your power?** Role model the behaviors you seek to develop in your students. Model workplace communication.

8. **Everyone is accountable for everything they do, so acknowledge mistakes!** Students are resilient if you step up and acknowledge your mistake, then move forward. The respect you will earn pays off in great dividends.

9. **Teach your students the power of advocating for themselves, as they will need to in real life.** "Could you please speak more slowly?" and "I feel I have earned a pay-level raise," sound like simple requests but are milestones of achievement for many students.

10. **Create a future of possibilities.** Relate your instruction to potential future opportunities.

11. **The better educated you *and* your students' parents are about their neurological challenges,** the greater the possibilities for success.

12. **Policies and procedures exist for a reason.** If you don't understand the reason, *ask*. It's what you would expect of your students.

TRAINING PARENTS IN TANDEM

The first and best teachers are parents, because they know their children better than we do. Regardless of how parents react to their children's learning struggles, or even what others might think of their parenting, we've never presumed to know more about any particular child than that child's parent does. It makes sense, then, to include parent training in this chapter on training those who teach TCS students. Early on, we understood that if we wanted to be a partner in a child's progress through life, we would need to walk side-by-side with his parents. Even speaking on the most basic terms, what sense would there be in building a child's self-esteem at school only to see it unintentionally torn down at home because we hadn't informed the parents about their child's need?

What sense would there be in building a child's self-esteem at school only to see it unintentionally torn down at home because we hadn't informed the parents about their child's need?

Of course, as the administrators of the school, we would routinely meet with parents one-on-one to clarify their student's issues, just as the teachers do. Teachers also adhere to a logged schedule of parent calls, to keep families apprised of progress and issues. (Teachers and principals communicate regularly with students' therapists and other attending professionals, as well, to ensure all efforts are coordinated.)

Because teachers routinely work beyond their one-on-one meetings and calls, and as class and school news and events march on relentlessly, a regular, robust communication system is essential. Wednesday packets are the solution, containing class and school updates, calendar items, things such as permission slips for upcoming trips (which might not make it home from class via a student), plus a note from the head of the school. Wednesday packets aggregate what, at another school, might be disparate communications: information from a math teacher on Monday, something from the social studies teacher on Tuesday, and so on. The once-a-week packet to parents makes it easy for them to stay connected with their child's needs for every class and the school as a whole. Parents agree, up front, to review the packet each Wednesday and to respond with what is needed back from them.

Perhaps the most significant parent-partnering effort we initiated is that of our educational evening sessions for parents, which mirror the visiting-expert sessions we provide for the faculty and staff. (Many times, educational opportunities are not planned in advance, but are arranged ad hoc when a teacher becomes aware that a parent or parents do not understand an issue that a child is facing.) Keeping the parents on the same exact page as our own teachers and staff is critical to TCS students' success. The Cottage School encourages all families to attend educational sessions; the insight is not only essential for parents of those children dealing with the conditions being discussed, but for their TCS classmates and, thus, their classmates' parents.

Larger meetings are eminently helpful to TCS parents. It is often comforting for parents to see that a presentation or discussion resonates with other parents. Then, they understand that they are not alone in their journeys with their children, or are not the only ones who have experienced a particular issue or faced fear for their child's future. It is common for parents to forge supportive relationships after educational evening meetings.

The school and teacher effort to keep parents connected is ongoing and managed via a documented system of checks and balances. Unconnected, a parent—the child's best teacher—would be unable to carry the baton of ongoing education and assistance at home. A significant portion of faculty training is dedicated to the critical aspect of parent connectedness. While teachers are trained to manage *over*-involved parents (parents who do their child's homework or nervously hound teachers about minutiae), TCS teachers seek to keep families involved in a productive way by encouraging an ongoing relationship through evening and one-on-one meetings, class and school gatherings and events, and attention to the Wednesday packets. Parents of children with neurological and behavioral issues may be either desperate to control the school situation after struggling with their children at home and in previous school environments, or they are exhausted from the battle and tend to relinquish involvement. TCS strives to restore both of these states to balance, through the thoughtfully designed parent-partnering joist of The Cottage School scaffold.

Five Takeaways

1. Teacher training (new teacher and ongoing) is the critical hub of the TCS program.

2. Ongoing professional development must target the needs of the faculty.

3. Faculty-to-faculty instruction reinforces the Culture of Safety, consistency of practice throughout the program, and an environment of mutual support.

4. Modeling desired behavior is a critical necessity for student growth.

5. Ongoing parent training serves to support all: students, teachers, and families.

CHAPTER THREE

ACCOUNTABILITY, SELF-ESTEEM, AND EMPOWERMENT

You can do anything in this world if you are
prepared to take the consequences.

**—W. Somerset Maugham, celebrated playwright,
novelist, and short story writer**

When we first interviewed Meghan at the Cottage School, she was a surly, uncommunicative tenth-grader fully decked out in black "goth" garb, complete with piercings. She slouched in her chair and peeled her black-painted nails while her parents spoke about her recent diagnoses of auditory processing deficits and depression. Then we turned the conversation directly to her.

"We can teach you all about these diagnoses and how they interfere with learning in a traditional school setting," we said. We explained that understanding her own neurology—and learning special "workarounds"—would help her manage any areas of weakness.

"But let's talk about positives first," we suggested, and asked, "What would you say are your greatest strengths?" She shrugged and remained silent, scowling at her nails.

After a moment or so, her mother piped up with, "We think Meghan has real acting ability—"

Meghan grumbled, "They mean a real strength. Acting's not a real strength, Mom."

On the contrary, we explained, acting was indeed a very real strength. Meghan exhaled dismissively.

"Well, if you don't feel you have any strengths to speak of," one of us interjected, "what would you say your weaknesses are?"

With that, Meghan sat up and proceeded to recite a list of weaknesses she had little trouble calling up (no doubt because they had been drilled into her during the previous decade or so): she was lazy, probably not smart enough for high school, did not listen or pay attention in class, did not turn in assignments on time, was rude and unfriendly, unhelpful at home, argumentative, sloppy, and uninterested in just about everything. She had a few friends but didn't like people anyway, she insisted.

We wish we had a nickel for every student ever interviewed at The Cottage School who could not conjure up a single strength, yet could easily rattle off a veritable catalogue of shortcomings.

We wish we had a nickel for every student ever interviewed at The Cottage School who could not conjure up a single strength, yet could easily rattle off a veritable catalogue of shortcomings. In fact, a focus on inadequacies is typical of special-needs students, many of whom have been fairly crushed by their unsuccessful experiences with mainstream education. Yet, this is also the case for a significant percentage of "typical" high schoolers as well, for adolescents are notoriously insecure about their skills and talents.[27] It is a rare teen, for instance, who can point to his ability to make friends as "solid people skills." Yet, people skills constitute a sought-after ability in almost any job market. What's more, they help to ensure a well-socialized individual and a happy life.

Meghan, as it turned out, had plenty of valuable skills and she developed them well. After The Cottage School, she went on to graduate from college and became the admissions director for her alma mater. One of her many skills in this regard is interviewing new generations of young people about *their* strengths, weaknesses, and life direction!

CREATING A THREE-STRAND CULTURE

On the face of it, the following statement may seem obvious: *No enterprise of any kind can flourish in a culture that impedes it.* Yet it is astounding how many workplaces are also homes to negative or non-supportive cultures which permeate everything. Why do we speak of "workplaces" when we are talking about The Cottage School? Simply because a school—where students industriously pursue education and educators strive to deliver that education—is a place of work, too!

In any school, both educators and students should work consistently toward their mutual goal of helping students to develop the innate skills, talents, and interests that will help them succeed in the

---

27 A simple Google search for "insecure teens" calls up countless articles and studies regarding "normal" teens' inability to view their strengths, while they are acutely aware of their liabilities.

real world beyond. It is essential that a school culture be specifically designed and then nurtured to be positive and supportive to its students. This is particularly true for The Cottage School, which serves learners who face roadblocks of many kinds. Our enrollees can come to us so defeated, they have diminished self-confidence, little sense of their ability to steer their own lives, and thus a limited understanding of their ownership of their actions. We therefore knew that the ideal culture for The Cottage School would be one that builds:

Our enrollees can come to us so defeated, they have diminished self-confidence, little sense of their ability to steer their own lives, and thus a limited understanding of their ownership of their actions.

- **Accountability**—The ability to be wholly responsible for one's commitments and accountable for commitments not met.

- **Self-esteem**—Confidence and pride in one's own abilities, whatever they may be.

- **Empowerment**—The ability to control one's own life and advocate for one's best interests.

The TCS culture is specifically designed to intertwine the three strands of accountability, self-esteem, and empowerment. Each of the three strands is as important as the next; together they form a fiber of tensile strength that can help our students weave a resilient life fabric, strong enough to support challenges to come.

Any parent would hope for this kind of learning culture for their child, but for neurologically and learning-challenged students, the three-strand culture is even more essential. *Accountability* can be critical for ADD/ADHD students who characteristically have trouble seeing the correlation between action and consequence. And for our students who have experienced repeated failure throughout their school years, self-esteem may be virtually non-existent, inhibiting any kind of advancement before it can even begin. In addition, most TCS students' previous experiences have been colored by a sense of powerlessness. But a culture that thrives on empowerment and teaches young people to speak up for themselves in a thoughtful, productive manner does more than energize study; it is life-empowering. Let's look more closely at these three strands:

Accountability

Because the TCS program "scaffold" is constructed around A) Pay Levels, B) the Individualized Education Plan, and C) the TCS program Planner, accountability is built into each and every goal and assignment, just as it is in the real world. These tools enable clear, observable, and measurable goals essential for achieving accountability—and thus, success.

Jon, for instance, is at Pay Level 2, and has worked hard to overcome his ADHD roadblocks to get there. He uses his planner to help him track the daily and weekly tasks he must complete on time, in accordance with the individual education plan (IEP) that he has created with the assistance of his parents and his homeroom teacher. Jon has learned that if he loses track of tasks, his teachers will not be able to sign off on a task not completed—just as an employer in the working world would not be able to OK a dropped responsibility to the company. He does not receive his anticipated pay for a missed task, just as a salesman would not receive any commission for a sale not closed. The missed pay is not punishment, it is "money" that might have gone toward an activity or exciting new elective, had he followed through on his commitment to himself to complete the task in furtherance of his IEP goals. Each and every day, Jon learns again and again (as he would in adult life) that he has a responsibility to keep commitments he has made or manage the consequences if he does not. On a daily basis, then, Jon internalizes the yin and yang of accountability.

SHOULD YOU PICK AND CHOOSE FROM TCS?

Today, there are certainly more special-needs schools adopting a life-skills, vocational, and experiential learning approach, and that's great news. We even know of a few schools that have attempted to institute a "paycheck" or "checkbook" system.

Yet when it comes to creating a behavioral system that works, cherry-picking from TCS (or any other successful unique learning environment) can backfire and do more harm than good. Here's why:

Any truly effective behavioral system must be based on the science of behavioral analysis (previously known as behavior modification). Applied behavioral analysis involves extremely specific dos and don'ts constructed around countless studies and decades of hands-on experience in the field. The many components of the TCS program, like other successful programs, incorporate thoroughly vetted research and results, and are interdependent.

So what happens if you decide to implement a "checkbook" concept, for instance, without understanding the intricate supporting structure of experiential learning for behavioral change? You've instituted pay-as-you-go *bribery*—certainly not the behavioral modification you were looking for!

Self-Esteem

Earning designated pay for work achieved is a constant and consistent reinforcement of growth. It organically builds self-esteem as TCS students progress through their class hours, days, and weeks, keeping their commitments. Ironically, overcoming pay-level setbacks can do just as much if not more to build pride and self-esteem; the accomplishment is that much greater after a slip.

Alicia had done well in algebra, and had been working hard this year to succeed in geometry. Still, with her innate visual-processing deficits, she struggled with each assignment. She just couldn't visualize the geometry problems in her homework tasks. Her math teacher had noted her difficulties and had worked with her in class to help her through the spatial-reasoning processes needed for the discipline. Alicia worried that she was holding up her classmates, even though—true to The Cottage School culture—her classmates mostly sought to help and support her.

Assignments were spread out to give Alicia additional time to work on them, and her teacher and parents spoke on the phone and then discussed alternatives with her, which included tutoring sessions after school, or even switching over to a math discipline more suitable to Alicia's skill set.

But her confidence was taking a hit. In self-protect mode, she soon neglected her homework assignment altogether rather than face up to her inability to understand it. Alicia felt the sting of her pay loss for the incomplete assignment, however, when she wasn't able to pay for an extracurricular activity she had been looking forward to. Finally, she took the uncomfortable step of asking her math and homeroom teachers to meet with her and her parents, to find a solution to the problem.

"I feel like such a failure," she told them. "Why can't I get geometry? Everyone else can!"

"Actually, not everyone *can* 'get' geometry," her homeroom teacher responded. "Sure, determination goes a long way when we tackle something that does not come naturally to us," she acknowledged. "But sometimes, we also have to know when to tweak our goals, rather than undermine our confidence so much that it affects our ability to operate well in the other areas of our life."

After discussion, Alicia realized that the decisions about the geometry class were hers alone. She would have to take responsibility for them. Weighing her options, she asked her math teacher if he would be willing to tutor her to bring her up to speed. The math teacher agreed to take on the extra work with a proviso: If, after a month of tutoring, the work still proved overwhelming, Alicia would move to a math alternative

Alicia realized that the decisions about the geometry class were hers alone. She would have to take responsibility for them.

that was less alien to her. Alicia agreed and worked hard in her tutoring sessions while her math teacher was able to come up with clever props and study aids to help her visualize the spatial concepts. One month later, Alicia was onboard with geometry and had caught up with her class.

"I did it! I defeated geometry!" Alicia announced to her homeroom teacher the day she "graduated" from her tutoring sessions. She penned a heartfelt thank-you to her math teacher and tutor, for all of the extra hours he had donated to her struggle. In return, she offered to share what she had learned with other students having trouble with geometry concepts.

Alicia had been faced with a dilemma that briefly sent her into an old self-protection pattern, but she faced the consequences, was accountable for her actions, risked an empowered decision, and prevailed. Her newfound levels of self-esteem were inestimable.

Empowerment

First and foremost for a TCS student, empowerment requires knowledge of personal neurology, the strengths on which to build, and the weaknesses to remediate. Then, throughout each day, TCS students are encouraged to act as their own best advocates. The immediate reward for controlled risk-taking is often well worth it—getting someone else to see your point of view, or taking on a challenge just outside of one's comfort zone, for instance.

Yet the real reward is the victory over powerlessness as young people learn to exercise their new muscles of self-knowledge and self-advocacy and become more and more empowered along the way. Looking at the example in the section above, Alicia's determination to learn how to accommodate her neurology and her decision to be her own advocate in her geometry-class challenge, contributed greatly to the self-esteem she gained from the experience.

TCS MIRRORS CAUSE AND EFFECT IN THE REAL WORLD

Sooner or later, most parents shudder at the ironic adage, "Do as I say, not as I do." At some point, they have to admit that it was probably devised as a lesson about the emptiness of parental words versus the power of modeling appropriate behavior for their children. They must face the truth: human beings model *behavior*, not lectures. A father who sermonizes about accepting consequences, yet finds someone to "fix" his speeding ticket, is teaching his daughter to shirk the consequences of her actions—a lesson she will live by. On the other hand, a mother who follows through on the promises she makes to family and friends teaches her son about integrity, trust, and the value of keeping commitments. In short, words do not teach cause-and-effect, experiences do.

The TCS three-strand culture is, above all else, *experiential.* Though it is based on concepts and words (our mission, our stated ten tenets,[28] and our shared values), the TCS culture is all about real-life experience: we *live* our tenets and values, through our behavior. It is not enough to say that TCS students should pay attention to their appearance, or strive to be punctual. Through the experience of concrete and immediate cause and effect, TCS tenets and behaviors become ingrained, and the TCS culture becomes self-perpetuating.

We believe that it is helpful for *anyone* to understand that, "if I do this, then this happens." Some young people are fortunate to have parents who instill in them the reality of consequences, and some have benefited from an education that also manages real-life experiences well. But the majority of the students who come to The Cottage School are, at the very least, confused about cause and effect. They often assume that if bad things happen to them, it must be someone else's fault; if good things happen to them, it must be a mistake or a fluke. As we've pointed out, ADD/ADHD students, in particular, struggle with the concept of cause and effect: they often pass tests they didn't study for, fail tests they did prepare for, get into trouble when they don't com-

> **We believe that it is helpful for anyone to understand that, "if I do this, then this happens."**

---

28   The ten TCS tenets are stated and discussed in chapter 1.

prehend what they did, or get away with something they shouldn't have.

To successfully move into adulthood, children of all ages need to understand the role they play in bringing about consequences in their lives. Everything embedded in the TCS culture helps our students clear up their misperceptions about their role in what does or does not happen in their lives and why. It makes the lines between cause and effect eminently clear. Because cause and effect is what happens in real life, TCS moves the real world into the classroom and into the culture that runs beneath everything we do.

We start with the five life-skills or job-readiness behaviors that run through the TCS culture and are posted in every classroom:

1. Punctuality

2. Being prepared for the task at hand

3. Communicating in an appropriate manner

4. Dressing appropriately

5. Completing tasks at hand

These skills may seem no-brainers to you but when you think about it, plenty of adults have never mastered one or more of the above skills. In fact, today's employers often complain that more recent generations of employees entering the workplace are noticeably lacking in basic job-readiness skills. (This may be why regional employers often tell us they *love* employing job-ready TCS graduates!)

In the TCS program, not completing homework (see #5 in the list above) is a non-judgmental black-and-white issue; it means that a student—any student—does not earn that portion of his or her hourly pay for work not turned in. And across our TCS culture, communicating in an inappropriate manner (see #3) is not tolerated because it is personally damaging to people and counterproductive, as well. That applies to a student blowing up at a classmate, or a teacher diminishing a student with a thoughtless or uncaring comment. Even tardiness (see #1) spins out multiple consequences. A student late for class (1) puts himself behind in the day's lesson, (2) disrupts the work of others, which can create a learning gap for them, too, which (3) causes the teacher to devote extra time to bring students up to speed.

Our students learn early on that modifying their behavior has consequences not just for themselves; it will cost *both parties to an action.* In the working world, an employer would soon respond negatively to infractions that would be costly on one level or another. Yet that same employer might willingly invest in a talented employee who requests additional training.

A cause-and-effect culture demonstrates for students that the real-life result of not learning to work with fractions can be as relevant as trying to divide three-quarters of a cup of sugar by fourths, to make six cupcakes instead of two dozen.

Thus, the cause and effect of life-skills behaviors (or the lack of them) suddenly makes school and academic study *relevant* for kids who can't fathom why they might ever need to know about division of fractions. A cause-and-effect culture demonstrates for students that the real-life result of not learning to work with fractions can be as relevant as trying to divide three-quarters of a cup of sugar by fourths, to make six cupcakes instead of two dozen.

ACHIEVING SUCCESS THROUGH THE INDIVIDUALIZED EDUCATION PLAN (IEP)

At the Cottage School, when we speak of success, what we are really talking about is our students' achievement of accountability, self-esteem, and empowerment. The levels of those achievements may vary—how much self-esteem, for instance, is enough? The answer to that question is: whatever is enough to work for the individual, to help her find her way in the world. That path may not be a conventional path; it only needs to be a path that works for the TCS student.

Take Wayne, for instance. Wayne was an Asian-American student who came to us in seventh grade markedly overweight, profoundly depressed, angry, and intransigent. He played computer war games obsessive-compulsively, sometimes for forty-eight hours straight. He would rarely attend school. He was a fully Americanized kid who lived with his Asian-born parents and grandparents, so entrenched in their native culture that he did not feel free to bring a schoolmate home. His father was hardworking and exacting, yet traveled much of the time; his mother was bright but deferential. No one in the family knew what to do with this oversized, often unpleasant child who had stopped participating in anything except computer combat.

When we first met Wayne, he shuffled his way into our offices wearing flip-flops and cloaked in a hoodie and skepticism. After some discussion about the general shape and form of his IEP, we could see that our mock-money pay scale would not serve as a powerful enough incentive for behavioral change where Wayne was concerned. A special IEP sidebar was needed.

"You love computers?" we said, "OK, for every hour you spend in class, prepared with your materials, and spending your time productively, we will create a half-hour of afternoon elective class time on the computer. But you have to get your work done in your morning classes. You don't have to lead the class, you just have to complete the work."

"I'm not socializing with anyone," he pronounced, and then shuffled his way out the door.

As he promised, Wayne was a real challenge. Many of our teachers' afternoon sessions served as venting time for the educators who worked with him. Wayne was consistently negative and downright mean at times, and would not work with psychologists. He never did get past his anger at his parents, who he banned from his graduation ceremony. But by the time he graduated, he had slimmed down and literally gotten with the program. It was clear that he was sharp as a tack and, beneath his cantankerousness, there ran a vein of dry wit. He could have found his calling as a stand-up comic, if nothing else.

As it happened, however, Wayne was the first TCS student to graduate from Georgia Tech. He was a computer expert and math whiz who had fairly ripped through his calculus studies. The computer-pay IEP sidebar had served both Wayne and his teachers well. Though he never did get past a Level Two pay scale, he didn't see Level Three as essential to what he needed to accomplish. Wayne knew himself well and the IEP he endorsed did its job.

FINDING AND BUILDING PERSONAL STRENGTHS

We believe that *all* students possess an unlimited potential for success in their communities, places of work, and the world at large. That means that young people impacted by their individual learning styles possess the same unlimited potential to uncover and express their abilities and talents as any other student. We created The Cottage

School to help each young person discover his or her potential, develop it, and employ it confidently in the world at large.

Yet often, this process is unintentionally sabotaged by parents who, initially, focus on their child's weaknesses. A father may pronounce his son inherently lazy, incorrigible, or "not up to the job" (equipped) to succeed in school or the workplace. Conversely, a mother may attempt to obscure her daughter's weaknesses to help her succeed in school. She will edit or correct homework or else complete a school project to make it "right."

But parents soon become comfortable with the TCS culture, designed to uncover and build on strengths, while managing those behaviors or issues which could hold their child back from progress (issues that, for lack of a better term, are referred to as weaknesses). When students and parents alike commit to the TCS culture of accountability, self-esteem, and empowerment, strengths suddenly start to surface and weaknesses become manageable. Perhaps the following excerpt from a parent's letter to us says it best:

> **When students and parents alike commit to the TCS culture of accountability, self-esteem, and empowerment, strengths suddenly start to surface and weaknesses become manageable.**

Dear Jacque and Joe,

… I had to let you know what a great year this has been for Tanner. For years, I had been searching and praying for just the right middle school. I always seemed to come up frustrated and scared for what was available. It never seemed quite the right fit for both the academic and social aspect. At the same time, Tanner was bright and needed to be challenged. I guess above all, the social aspect of attending a public school was just too gut wrenching for me to even think about. Because Tanner was ready for sixth grade, my husband suggested that we [visit] The Cottage School and see if it would be a fit ...

To fast forward, this year has been one of growth and overcoming hurdles. I thank you and *all* of your staff for working with Tanner and seeing him as an individual with unique talents and abilities to uncover. I can see so much progress in him through self-esteem, accountability, and improved social interaction as well ... Everyone has been a major influence on his growth and loving to get up in the morning to go to a school. I want to thank Phil for giving Tanner the opportunity to learn to love art and to show what he is capable of ... No words can be enough to say thank you!

Very truly yours,

[Name withheld for privacy]

CREATING A SENSE OF COMMUNITY

While creating and fostering a culture of accountability, self-esteem, and empowerment forged the foundation upon which the TCS scaffold rests, a very real sense of community is the glue and nails that keeps the culture strong and vibrant. Every TCS student, for instance, takes ownership in the TCS community by performing a campus-related job. This teaches students that their individual and personal responsibility to maintaining our campus is an important contribution. All students know that they are no longer isolated, but part of a group. Everyone's role matters and the community would miss them, were they not there to contribute to the whole.

Bi-monthly pay-level meetings (where students are raised to their next pay level and interact based on their performance success and goals) also help build community. In the meetings, students learn to advocate for themselves and discuss their goals and progress (or lack of progress) with each other prior to the all-hands votes on individual raises. Students who do not support an individual's raise must clearly state their well-considered reasoning. The pay-level meeting is a specially modeled environment, and the students and the teachers assisting the process are highly trained. In thirty years, the pay-level meeting has always served as a powerful and positive experience for students—one that binds the community together.

We also look to our students to come up with programs or everyday solutions to issues before us. We prod our students to advocate for themselves and one another by asking them, "What do you think we need to do to fix this problem?" Sharing the mantle of responsibility to improve the TCS experience always helps create community.

One cannot underestimate the role that the five life-skills (listed in the section above) play in the strength of our TCS community, which encompasses students, parents, and staff. Communicating in an appropriate manner, for one, means that all community members are safe to be who they are, express what they need to express, and ask for what they need. The strict adherence to the other four life-skills means that everyone can count on everyone else to do their best, keep commitments to one another, represent themselves and the school well, and be proud of their accomplishments.

Five Takeaways

1. The three-strand culture of accountability, self-esteem, and empowerment is at the core of the TCS program.

2. Clear, observable, and measurable goals are essential for accountability and thus for achieving success.

3. Understanding personal strengths is essential in establishing areas for growth and building self-esteem.

4. Empowerment requires self-advocacy plus knowledge of one's neurology and the accommodations required to remediate areas of weakness.

5. Cause-and-effect relationships must be concrete and immediate.

6. Modifying behavior (at least initially) will cost all parties involved.

CHAPTER FOUR

THE POWER OF TEAMING CURRICULUM WITH LIFE-SKILLS LEARNING

I really believe that everyone has a talent, ability, or skill
that he can mine to support himself and succeed in life.

—Dean Koontz, bestselling suspense and science fiction author

We learned early on in our teaching careers that every child—no matter his or her neurological, developmental, social, or family situation—has strengths that, uncovered, nurtured, and developed, can steer that child confidently into adulthood and through life. That is success. We believe absolutely that the best way to accomplish the development of those strengths is through the consistent and systematic teaching of academic and essential life-skills combined. The TCS program facilitates this unique educational delivery by placing it in the milieu in which our students will be utilizing their education to support themselves, and in which they will be demonstrating their independence and ability to persevere in the proving ground of life: the workplace.

THE BUSINESS COMMUNITY SPEAKS

When we began formulating the structure of The Cottage School, we heard from members of the business community that their greatest challenge was finding employees who were prepared to be *successful* employees. Business leaders we spoke with admitted that they didn't know how they could effectively change their young new employees' inadequate behavior. Moreover, they weren't sure what would have been needed to prepare students for the demands of the workplace. Their concerns extended not just to high school students seeking part-time employment, but to college graduates entering the job market as well.

It seemed that the new employees had problems arriving at work on time or communicating in advance that they were going to be late due to unforeseen circumstances. These young hires had little sense of the negative impact of not reporting for work, often explaining absences after the fact—something that may have been tolerated in college. Task deadlines also appeared to be problematic for many of the new hires. After all, teachers and professors had often granted extensions, or else parents had zealously monitored homework and assignments to ensure turn-in dates weren't missed.

Young hires had little sense of the negative impact of not reporting for work, often explaining absences after the fact—something that may have been tolerated in college.

Dressing appropriately was another employer area of concern, and not just for workers in customer-facing positions. As students, the young employees had been expressing themselves through faddish or group identity attire (e.g., geek, gamer, rocker, goth, hipster, etc.). They had sported flip-flops, tattoos, assorted body piercings, and outlandish or unkempt hair fashions for years. Or, they had simply been unconcerned with the concept of dressing thoughtfully for a particular activity or milieu, wearing anything comfortable enough for sleep, recreation, or relaxation. Modes of dress did not always change much once they entered the job market.

Communication skills, too, were a real sticking point. Employers found themselves dealing with young people who, when frustrated or displeased, could exhibit tantrum-like or abusive behavior. Others were uncommunicative or simply arrived at work "in a bad mood," which affected not just their own productivity, but efficiency all the way down the line. Finally, many managers were confounded when employees simply failed to deliver on tasks instead of discussing stumbling blocks with managers. Often, managers did not discover that young hires were unprepared to tackle specific tasks—skills for which their manager could have offered training—until after deadlines went unmet.

High-profile parents (fathers, especially) of potential TCS enrollees frequently shared stories with us about the behaviors exhibited by some of their younger employees. They were frustrated by the amount of time they and their managers needed to spend trying to establish appropriate workplace behaviors for new hires. They hoped that their own children would not tread the same path. Months or years later, as their own progeny entered the workforce well prepared, they were greatly relieved that their TCS student son or daughter would have the advantage of career choices unhampered by the same kind of employer angst. As HR guru, philanthropist, and InfoMart founder Tammy Cohen put it so well, "A great employee is like a four-leaf clover, hard to find and lucky to have." What parent would not want his or her child to be equally as valuable to the working world?

THE FIFTEEN EMPLOYEE TRAITS AN EMPLOYER EXPECTS*

Most of us assume that job performance is all-important. But many personal traits can certainly get in the way of job execution, and managers will tell you that employees have lost their positions or surrendered advancement opportunities for reasons other than performance of duties. Depending upon the enterprise in which an individual works, many other traits could figure prominently. In a fitness club, for instance, good health and fitness might move up the list. For a software employer, teamwork skills could be critical. In a legal or financial environment, confidentiality may be paramount. What traits might be essential in a customer-facing post, or in a position in which the young or elderly rely on the consistency of daily services?

1. If you are an employer or manager, or if you can imagine yourself one, rank the following employer expectations in order of importance, with one most important and fifteen least important. (You may add and rank any personal qualities you might desire that are not listed.)

2. Then—and this is just as important—go back and put an X next to the traits you would be able to do without.

3. Finally, if you are a parent, or you can imagine yourself one, go back and put a ✓ next to the life-skills you believe your child could succeed without.

Adapted from "What Your Employer Expects: Personal Qualities on the Job," reprinted with permission of Goodheart-Wilcox publishers, and arranged in alphabetical order.

_____ confidentiality

_____ cooperation

_____ courtesy

_____ excellent job performance

_____ good attendance

_____ good health and fitness

_____ honesty

_____ initiative

_____ loyalty

_____ neat personal appearance

_____ positive attitude

_____ punctuality

_____ receptive to constructive criticism

_____ strong work ethic

_____ teamwork skills

LIFE-SKILLS IN A CONCRETE, NON-JUDGMENTAL ENVIRONMENT

In the TCS model, the life-skills needed to succeed in both the workplace and life in general are not subjective, but black-and-white requirements for all members of the TCS community, students and staff alike. Simply put, they are requirements in The Cottage School because they are requirements in life. The years spent in mainstream schools often serve to create disconnect between practices tolerated in high school or on a college campus and the reality of what is expected in the working world. The Cottage School model was created to eliminate that confusion and make the way the world works crystal clear.

> **The years spent in mainstream schools often serve to create disconnect between practices tolerated in high school or on a college campus and the reality of what is expected in the working world.**

Learning to Be On Time

In the working world, punctuality applies to more than an employee's daily arrival at a place of business; it extends to every facet of a workday. Have the reports been completed on time? Did the trucks ship out on time with the promised merchandise? Did the meeting go off as scheduled? Were customers or important accounts met at the designated time and place?

Punctuality may seem like the most no-brainer facet of employee responsibility, but if you Google "employees not on time," the following article headlines will give you a very real sense of the levels of frustration experienced by today's employers:

- "Never on Time: How to Handle a Perpetually Late Employee" —The Muse

- "How to Get Millennial Employees to Show Up to Work on Time" —*Inc.*

- "7 Steps for Getting the Chronically Late Employee to Be Punctual" —*Entrepreneur*

- "Dealing With an Employee Who Is Always Late" —Natural HR

- "What Can You Do to Reduce Employee Time Theft?" —The Balance Careers

Students with neurological, developmental, and social-emotional issues often have the most valid reasons for losing track of time; they do not process time-keeping in the same manner as students who don't struggle with such issues. But these same young people still need to make their way in their world and find success and fulfillment. What's so ironic is how well-prepared our TCS graduates are to be punctual, when so many of their mainstreamed peers are not!

Teaching punctuality to TCS students begins with the start of the TCS workday. With a real-world "clocking in" time card (later, fingerprint scan) system, our students are either on time and earn their pay for the full day of school, or they do not. Classroom attendance is a function of the school-wide bell system: students are at their desks, planners out, and materials ready to begin class when the bell rings, or they risk losing a portion of that class time pay.

Students are at their desks, planners out, and materials ready to begin class when the bell rings, or they risk losing a portion of that class time pay.

A sick-leave policy allots each student eight hours of discretionary leave each marking period to manage tardies and absences. If the student (not the parent or anyone else) calls in to indicate he or she may be late or will be absent, the tardy or absence is deducted from sick leave. Once a sick-leave allotment is spent, any subsequent time away from school must be made up the afternoon of the tardiness or 7:00 a.m. the morning following an absence, per the time clock. For students who find themselves in a hole at the end of the six-week marking period, the make-up day is 8:00 a.m. Saturday. Students, parents (who drive their children to the early make-up sessions), and teachers (who monitor the early-morning sessions), each pay a price for the transgression.

Still, as we have said, behavior modification always bears a cost to all involved. In the workforce, where an employer won't stand for repeated absences, the cost is borne by more than just the offender who finds himself out of a job. The employer is minus an employee and now has to scramble to replace or fill-in the post, and any partner or spouse of the transgressor will probably have to struggle (not willingly or happily) with the hardship that the lack of income generates. Much better to learn earlier in life to arrive as required! TCS students grasp quickly that they cannot be successful in life if they don't show up prepared and on time.

Modeling Appropriate Workplace Attire Through Dress Code

We could go into extensive detail here about our TCS dress code iterations over the years as we weighed the importance of appropriateness against the inevitable adolescent desire to express individuality and creativity. At times, many students—and even their parents—insisted our dress code was unreasonable. They often pushed hard for school uniforms (as many private schools employ), to take the angst out of the morning dressing-for-school fracas.

But we made it clear, time and again that, whatever the dress code was, it was up to the *students* to take responsibility for meeting it by choosing the appropriate garb for specific activities to ensure their hourly pay. Otherwise, it was up to them to create a legitimate, well-considered case for modifying the existing code—self-advocacy in action.

We pointed out time and again that young people must acquire the life skill of determining for themselves the appropriate attire for specific activities and events. To do that, they would need to practice the skill (and sometimes fail at it). Additionally, we explained, learning to choose style, color, accessories, etc., is an important part of balancing individuality with appropriateness. These were skills that would prove important in life after The Cottage School. If an individual were to lose a job opportunity because of a negative impression made by inappropriate dress, that circumstance should be a result of an individual's informed (if not miscalculated) choice, not because he or she didn't know any better.

Over time—and often by way of effective lobbying by our students—we modified the dress code to reflect cultural changes in the workplace. (Remember: TCS is modeled on the workplace, not on a typical mainstream school environment.) Neither Apple nor IBM served as our model. Cottage School males are required to wear collared shirts tucked into belted trousers; females can wear slacks or skirts with blouses. No shorts, t-shirts, exposed midriffs, or flip-flops.

The issue was not so much fairness as it was reality. The Cottage School was a workplace that would be like so many others TCS kids would head to after graduation. Would our students enhance their chances for success in the world by knowing how to operate within the workplace? Or would they (unwittingly or not) shoot themselves in the foot all through their important first years in the real world, simply because they had not acquired the fundamental life-skills that would allow them to focus on the most important aspects of their lives: their talents, skills, dreams, and aspirations?

Developing Appropriate Communication Skills

In mainstream educational settings, students with a history of failure learn early on that explosively expressed frustration gets the teacher's attention, while the students who play by the rules and are eager to learn, sit by. But in the TCS program, students are provided safety valves through which to safely vent frustration and thus avoid explosive behavior. They are counseled (not lectured!) that volatile behavior creates an unsafe environment for their classmates, thus it is inappropriate, self-serving, rude, and unacceptable. TCS students come to understand that out-of-control behavior cannot possibly earn them full pay—whereas the use of appropriate expression can. We also employ specialized role-playing and situational training for teachers who could, under stress, resort to comments they would never use when speaking to peers.

Being able to communicate an opposing viewpoint in a courteous fashion, or advocate for oneself in a challenged atmosphere, is a highly valuable skill not just for the workplace, but for wide-ranging success in life.

We school our students in advanced communication skills as well. For example, those more subtle skills involved in appropriately communicating work readiness. Being able to properly and effectively communicate an absence or tardiness in a timely fashion is essential in the TCS program because it is essential in life. Being able to communicate an opposing viewpoint in a courteous fashion, or advocate for oneself in a challenged atmosphere, is a highly valuable skill not just for the workplace, but for wide-ranging success in life.

Being Prepared for, and Completing, the Tasks at Hand

When employers speak of work ethic, being properly prepared for tasks and completing them in the anticipated manner (accountability), are top of mind. Enthusiasm (passion for the job) and ethical behavior on the job also top the employer's wish list but—let's face it—a worker who cannot come to the table prepared or get the job done fails the first job. TCS, designed within a workplace milieu, incorporates task preparation and task completion skills into every student's daily routine. The program planner assists students in acquiring and internalizing organizational skills as rote. Teachers, coaches, and non-academic instructors augment the process with written memos regarding any special preparation or materials needed for upcoming classes, and students learn to add these items to their planning agendas to prevent essentials from slipping through the cracks (and to avoid asking a parent to make a last-minute Walmart run and thus "pay" for a student's own organizational slip). The life mantra is: *write it down and check your planner, or lose your pay!*

TOP TEN TIPS FOR WORKPLACE SUCCESS WITH ADD/ADHD*

Mastering basic workplace and life-skills is as essential for ADD/ADHD students as it is for any young person—it just involves extra thought, planning, and preparation to develop good habits. The following skills can be ingrained through the consistent and repetitive practice and will help to ensure success in any suitable work environment:

*Adapted from *ADD in the Workplace: Choices, Changes, and Challenges* by Kathleen G. Nadeau, PhD.[29]

1.   Minimize paperwork to maximize success.

2.   De-stress to avoid distress.

3.   To arrive on time, plan to be early.

4.   Simplify your filing system.

5.   Do it now, or write it down.

6.   Negotiate for tasks that call on your strengths.

7.   Schedule interruption-free time blocks.

8.   Focus on ADD/ADHD *solutions*, not ADD/ADHD problems.

9.   Get everything in writing; don't depend on your memory.

10. Focus on task completion—no loose strings!

THE IMPORTANCE OF LEISURE TIME ACTIVITIES

People often forget that "life-skills" include skills we pick up or gravitate to in life that are outside of academic or work-defined skills. Often, those are skills we demonstrate during our "leisure" time, such as those we utilize for hobbies, recreation, sports, and the like. As educators working with children who display endless kinds of previously unearthed skills and talents, we always wonder why non-

---

29   Kathleen G. Nadeau, *ADD in the Workplace: Choices, Changes, and Challenges* (London: Routledge, 1998).

88

academic life-skills are so easily dismissed. We consider the millions of celebrated individuals who have led happy, dimensional, productive, and even financially rewarding lives, utilizing life-skills as opposed to strictly academic or business-based skills. We think of Picasso, Bill Gates, Tiger Woods, Paul McCartney, Meryl Streep, Jerry Seinfeld, Mario Andretti, Ralph Lauren—no slouches among them.

As educators working with children who display endless kinds of previously unearthed skills and talents, we always wonder why non-academic life-skills are so easily dismissed.

And we think of Jed. Jed came to us in middle school, an invisible overweight kid who had neurological issues (ADHD and/or Asperger's), but who also didn't want to risk anything by putting himself out there. He had no sense of his own value, and so trolled under the radar to stay safe. No one ever knew what was going on in his head. Jed's parents were frustrated because they were convinced that a child with interests and the passion to pursue them was trapped inside somewhere; they just didn't know how to help Jed emerge.

Pumping up the leisure-activity side of Jed's IEP did the trick. The Cottage School has a solid track and field program and, possibly because Jed's dad was a runner, Jed decided to test it out. That test revealed that Jed was a runner too. In fact, he amazed everyone with his speed. The accolades he received helped to build his confidence, which soon extended to the other areas of learning and socio-emotional development as he began participating in class. Self-esteem, empowerment, and accountability soared and soon everyone knew that there was plenty going on inside Jed's head; he had interesting thoughts about a lot of things! Jed went on to hold a number of Georgia State records in track and field, and graduated as a TCS rock star. When he visits The Cottage School today, he brings track and field event t-shirts for the coach, and is always asked to autograph them. Jed may not have decided to make his career in sports, but there is no doubt that his involvement in his afternoon leisure activities changed his life and helped to ensure it is rich and rewarding. Today, Jed is a supervisor in a niche construction company building supports for structures and piers.

At The Cottage School, the daily afternoon leisure activities are not only a great stress reliever (an outlet, we might add, that mainstream schools have largely eliminated). Leisure activities have helped so many of our students develop solid life-skills and even find their calling. Students can take whatever activities that they can propose and we can develop instruction for: carpentry, jewelry making, culinary arts, horseback riding—you name it. It often surprises us how many of our female graduates have gone into equine careers, for instance, and how many students have pursued successful livelihoods in fields such as construction, art, and music. We have, in fact, schooled a number of successful musicians—one a Grammy-nominated composer and producer, and another who is a guitarist, music producer, and Grammy winner.

CARING ABOUT COMMUNITY

When it comes to life-skills learning, few experiential lessons carry as much impact as learning to serve the community in which we live and work. That can mean our school community, our local or regional community, or the community at large: our fellow men, women, and children. This holds true for all young people, whether they are learning-challenged or not. Experiencing the reward of helping others, and pulling oneself *out* of oneself, is especially important for those with neurological, social, or developmental challenges. These young people are even more self-focused than most, because of the many challenges they face daily. Focusing on others brings great relief from self-consciousness, and imparting hard-earned knowledge to others achieves something magical for the special-needs student: all at once she becomes the instructor, not the instructed—a marker of great personal success! Few things do more for a young person's self-esteem. Thus, caring about community benefits both the special-needs helper and those helped.

TCS students are consistently encouraged to volunteer their time in community-based activities. The Cottage School student council has been involved in the national Adopt-a-Road program, with student body members conducting litter patrol in Roswell. Students routinely visit local nursing homes and provide patients with small personal care packages. Our volunteers pitch in at Roswell's Drake House for Social Services and tutor Hispanic students at the Star House Foundation (also in Roswell), where they read to teach young ESL[30] students. Not surprisingly, working at Star House is a favorite community activity, and improves the reading skills of TCS "tutors" while it improves those of their pupils! Many of our student tutors have reported that the experience of teaching others what they have learned is life-altering for them. The confidence they gain is an undeniable indicator that they have achieved success.

> **Many of our student tutors have reported that the experience of teaching others what they have learned is life-altering for them.**

---

30   English as a Second Language

SUCCESS BUILDS SUCCESS

"Once students taste success, they blossom into students and then leaders," Joe loves to say, and he's right: for nothing breeds success like success. We've watched our middle schoolers construct a pyramid in the middle of their classroom and then want to find out everything they can about ancient civilizations. We've witnessed our high schoolers tackle a daunting wall-climbing challenge—while helping each other over the top. These seemingly small moments are huge to our students who could not have completed their academic and experiential tasks without learning life-skills such as punctuality, preparedness, solid communication skills, appropriate attire for the job at hand, and caring about others (community).

To build success upon success, we use a very broad brush. Wherever we can find success for a student, we highlight it, capitalize on it, and use it as a springboard for a student to develop that confidence. We encourage our kids to try in areas that they previously thought, "There's no sense in trying because I'm going to fail anyway." We don't separate academic success and participation in extracurricular activities such as sports, for instance, the way a mainstream school would. ("If you get a D in algebra, you're benched!") We believe that if the only thing a kid excels at is basketball, he's going to be on the team. His success on the basketball court will help him build relationships with fellow students and coaches, and he will try harder in the classroom *because* of that success. He will certainly have the confidence to try harder than if his school excludes him from participating in the activity in which he is skilled and passionate.

The broad-brush approach also helps to create better teachers because most academic instructors only get to see one side of a student's personality—the failing math student, let's say. But if that teacher is also the basketball coach who experiences the same child shining on the court, then when they both are back in the classroom, that teacher has impetus for saying, "You can do this. Let's try it another way." The teacher will be more resilient and have more patience with a child she could have dismissed as she moved on to another student.

Five Takeaways

1. Help students and teachers work together to identify areas of student success.

2. Provide the structure required to build successful behaviors.

3. Encourage teachers to serve in both academic and non-academic roles.

4. Enhance academic efforts through extracurricular success.

5. Ensure the ratcheting-up of areas for success.

CHAPTER FIVE

THE SCHOOL/PARENT/ TEACHER PARTNERSHIP

*If you judge a fish by its ability to climb a tree, it will
live its whole life believing that it is stupid.*

—Anonymous

We have spoken at great length about how we reacted to our own experiences working with special-needs versus mainstream students as we progressed in our teaching careers. We have discussed how The Cottage School approaches its teaching, learning, and everyday interactions with its students. We have detailed what TCS teacher and staff training entails. We have even looked at the issue of untraining TCS teachers who come to us with unhelpful attitudes or previously acquired skill sets that are not aligned with our TCS mission and values.

Yet, children with special-learning needs (and all children, in fact) are not just impacted by their educators, they are also greatly influenced, for better or worse, by others they must interact with in their daily lives—friends, service providers and, most importantly, family members. Unfortunately, the best-intentioned parents may be unknowingly undermining the very progress they so ardently wish for, for their learning-challenged children. Parents of special-needs kids expend so much energy simply trying to coexist with their youngsters, it is common for them to lose their focus somewhere along the way. Even parents of children with no apparent learning roadblocks admit that child-rearing is a more complex and demanding challenge than they had ever dreamed. What parent could not use a parent-child "reset" specifically created to re-open doors that somehow keep slamming?

> **Unfortunately, the best-intentioned parents may be unknowingly undermining the very progress they so ardently wish for, for their learning-challenged children.**

When we think of the many parents who have brought their children to our offices for an initial interview over the years, we realize that a significant percentage of those parents had a distorted sense of their role in their child's progress.

FATHERS AS SKEPTICS

George and Tim

George, for instance, only enrolled his tenth-grade son, Tim, in The Cottage School reluctantly, after our interview. He simply wasn't convinced that investing the cost of tuition in Tim would be worth it. He described Tim as unmotivated and lacking in accountability—traits that were particularly hard for him to swallow not just as a father, but as a successful small business owner. Though we discussed

Tim's diagnosis of ADHD, George insisted that he knew his son well and the boy was *choosing* not to cooperate with everything they had previously tried. George complained that even the simplest responsibilities were a battle. Tim would not complete his homework without endless prompts, and was rarely prepared to leave the house on time for school. He doubted that sending Tim to yet another school would make much of a difference to his recalcitrant son.

Mike and Katherine

Mike, an IT executive, did not attend his daughter Katherine's initial interview at The Cottage School with her mother, Marge. Encouraged by the first meeting, Marge requested a second visit and we urged her to come back with her husband. When we met again—this time with Mike in tow—he stressed that while Katherine, a ninth grader with undiagnosed math and reading issues, was passing her classes in her mainstream school, she was performing well below the capabilities both parents knew she had, and her attitude was deplorable. "She just doesn't have any ambition," Mike insisted. Both parents had hoped to see some passion for learning from a daughter they were convinced was bright, but burying her talents.

Bill and Harry

Bill presented a commanding figure during our interview with his son, Harry, an eleventh grader who was failing his classes at a local high school. We thought we had heard every father's skeptical viewpoint when Harry and his parents arrived for our meeting, but Bill surprised us with a new one: if he enrolled Harry at The Cottage School, he pointed out, it would only be the *tuition payments* that would be responsible for any improvement in Harry's grades; the improvement would not indicate that any real learning had taken place. If Harry did not master his classes, he explained, the family would, in effect, only be *purchasing* Harry's grades. And Harry, he said, had no interest in real learning. So what would be the point of a full year of tuition when he could purchase less expensive just-passing grades for Harry by hiring a couple of tutors?

MOTHERS AS ENABLERS

There are endless iterations of skeptical dads, but they generally come around quickly once they see the progress being made (more about this in the following section). Yet, many mothers who enter our offices with their sons and daughters tend to fall into one catch-all category: that of the hovering mom.

That makes sense, for the very nature of mothering means that moms are watchful, nurturing trouble-shooters who feel responsible for their child's life experiences simply because, in the earliest years, that was their role: to fix skinned knees, patch a broken heart, or help with daunting school projects. In other words, to protect and serve. That role is tough to surrender as the years go by. So, even when an older child is suffering, it is frequently the mother who feels most responsible to address the situation.

For many of our new enrollees, the mother has been running interference for years and finds it impossible to suddenly trust her child's physical and emotional safety to strangers.

Aside from this sweeping statement about mothers and their children in general, it is certainly not surprising that mothers of special-needs kids, especially, become hoverers. For many of our new enrollees, the mother has been running interference for years and finds it impossible to suddenly trust her child's physical and emotional safety to strangers. In the previous school environment, this mom found ways to know what was going on nearly every minute of the day. She would email and text her child's teacher to suggest, question, advocate, and battle, if necessary.

Enterprising mothers of children who experience learning difficulties at an early age often adopt the role of "favorite room mother" so they can be around constantly to intervene, support, and manage their child's school experience. They ingratiate themselves with the teacher so that, should their child's behavior get out of hand, the teacher would be less inclined to reject or punish. In a mainstream educational setting not designed to focus on a child with special needs, we have to ask: What other choices does a caring mother of a special-needs child feel she has?

In a school specifically designed to foster independence and self-reliance, however, new choices are suddenly available. That does not mean that the hovering mom has an easy time suddenly dropping the behaviors that have protected her child previously. (When siblings are involved, the overly protective nature of the hovering parent of a special-needs child becomes even more complicated.)

When a hovering mom enrolls her child in a school that fosters independence and self-reliance, she often faces an unexpected identity crisis that cuts to her core. Even if she intellectually understands that severing the invisible umbilical cord will result in more confidence and happiness for her child, surrendering her role as protector can be excruciating. The most well-meaning mother may unconsciously resist no longer being needed all the time.

Sarah and Charles

Sarah, who came to us as the mother of Charles, a sixth grader with Asperger's syndrome, was the epitome of the hovering "room mother" mom. Each morning when she dropped Charles off at The Cottage School, she leapt out of the car and helped her son gather himself, his book bag, and his lunch. Then she knelt on the sidewalk beside him, hugged him, tucked in his shirt, straightened his collar, rubbed his shoulders, and repeatedly kissed him while those in the car line behind them got on with drop-off. The other students walked maturely and confidently by Charles and his mother, ready to proceed with their day. On some level, Charles had to know that the scene with his mom each morning set him apart from his peers.

When Joe attempted to discuss the issue with Sarah and explain why she needed to tone down the motherly demonstration each morning, she became incensed. She also consistently questioned her son's school assignments. They were alternately too difficult for him or not challenging enough for his talents. Although TCS required strict adherence to the school's policy of children completing their own homework, it was clear that Sarah was handling her son's assignments for him. Because she so often helped him complete his schoolwork, Charles's teachers had no idea if he was actually learning the material. (Prevention of such obfuscation was the purpose of the TCS "no homework help" rule.) Suggestions that Sarah end her son's nightly homework support infuriated her, and so teachers and staff were forced to work double-time to keep the relationship with Sarah from becoming downright toxic.

ELEVEN PARENTAL HANG-UPS THAT CAN SABOTAGE STUDENT SUCCESS

The list below is adapted from the National Institute of Mental Health.[31] As educators of unique learners, and many with neurological and other diagnoses, we have experienced every one of these parental concerns or behaviors that can sabotage a child's eventual success. Our goal is always to transfer the energy expended on some of these extremely ingrained behaviors, to a new set of concerns and behaviors: *OK, so he's got learning disabilities. What I can do to help? How can I make him better about himself? What are his strengths? What are his interests? Yes, it will take some time and cooperative effort, but I know that we will make it!*

1. **Denial.** My child doesn't really have anything wrong with him. He only needs more time, more understanding neighbors, a better teacher, a better school. These people don't understand him. He's just the way I was. There's basically nothing wrong. *Everyone* has one child who sucks the air out of a room!

2. **Flight.** These doctors jump to conclusions. We're going to see another specialist. They're only out to make more money with more tests and more examinations. We have to fly to the East (or the West, etc.) where there's a new specialist with a better reputation.

3. **Isolation.** Why doesn't anyone care? Nobody seems to understand. Why can't they make

---

31   Hilda Fried, and Sally Liberman Smith, *Plain Talk about Children with Learning Disabilities* (Rockville, MD: National Institute of Mental Health, Division of Scientific and Public Information, 1979).

allowances? She's much more interesting and unique than most children!

4. **Guilt.** What did I do to him? Why is God punishing me? How could I have made life better for him? If only I hadn't let him bump his head (catch measles, get that virus, etc.). If only I had been more careful, stricter, more caring, more watchful ...

5. **Anger.** Doctors don't know anything! They should have caught it earlier! That teacher is out of her mind! These psychologists are for the birds! I hate this neighborhood! That child makes a monkey out of me!

6. **Blame.** You baby her! You're the one who spoils her! You don't make her take responsibility! We never had anything like this on *our* side of the family.

7. **Fear.** Maybe it's worse than they say. Is he permanently *damaged* and they won't tell me? Does he have a progressive disease that will get worse? Will he ever be able to marry, have children, or hold a job?

8. **Envy.** Look at those other kids. They don't know how lucky they are. Everything comes easy to them. How did they become so popular? We're better parents than their parents. It's not fair!

9. **Bargaining.** Maybe she'll be OK if we move. Maybe she'll do just fine in third grade. Maybe if we send her to camp, she'll shape up. Maybe if she gets to visit her grandparents, she'll perk up. Maybe if ...

10. **Depression.** I've failed him. I'm no good. No wonder he can't make it; I can't either. The

world's no good. I'm no good. There's no hope for us.

11. **Mourning.** Think what could have been. She might have ...

WHAT HAPPENS TO TCS STUDENTS WHEN PARENTS SABOTAGE PROGRESS?

Most parents who impede their children's progress do so *unwittingly* but, even so, their misplaced good intentions don't serve to help their child—and help is the reason they enroll their children in the TCS program in the first place! To see what becomes of TCS enrollees with skeptical fathers and hovering mothers, for instance, let's take a look at the students discussed in the sections above, and find out what happened to them.

George and Tim: Taking Care of "Business"

Tim was the tenth grader diagnosed with ADHD, whose father, George, doubted that yet another school would make much of a difference to his son. George had insisted that Tim was stubbornly resisting learning. Yet, even as early on as the initial interview, as the structure of the TCS program was carefully detailed, Tim's father mentioned that he liked the accountability built into the TCS system. George began to appear more interested in the program as the discussion progressed. He told us that he especially appreciated the cause-and-effect relationship within our financial "workplace" structure. He hoped it would have a beneficial effect on his son.

Not long after Tim was enrolled, George told us that he was astonished by his son's change in attitude toward learning and responsibility. Tim was not only completing his homework without endless prompts, he was also prepared and ready to leave the house each morning so he would be on time for clock-in at school. His father confided he saw behavioral changes in Tim he never thought possible. (Tim went on to become head of one of the marketing departments at a large, international corporation.)

Mike and Katherine: Eyes Opened

While Mike had not attended his daughter Katherine's initial interview at The Cottage School, he appeared at a second meeting to point out that Katherine was an under-performer. Yet, Katherine revealed to us that she was very interested in the financial (Pay Level) aspect of the program. She wanted to know all about the hourly pay and her checking and savings accounts. When her father noted her interest in earning "money" for accomplishing hourly tasks, he agreed to try a year at The Cottage School.

Mike called us after Katherine's first month at school. "What have you done with my daughter?" he asked. Katherine was actively functioning at home as she had not been for several years; she was not only doing her school work and taking an interest in her classes, she was volunteering to assist with household chores! Not long after, Katherine began to talk about what she was planning to do after graduation. Katherine's parents reported that they were seeing a light in their daughter's eyes they thought had been extinguished. Mike and Marge went on to become two of our strongest

Cottage School parent partners throughout their daughter's enrollment and even well after graduation. Katherine graduated from college and currently teaches at a local elementary school.

Bill and Harry: Worth the Private School Investment?

Bill was convinced he would only be "purchasing" his son Harry's grades were he to enroll him in a private school. He wanted Harry to not just stop failing his high-school classes; he wanted his son to knuckle down, *master* his classes, and do his schoolwork the way Harry's siblings were able to. Bill believed that getting his act together might be painful for Harry, but necessary, if he was going to make his way in the world. He didn't trust independent schooling and assumed it would only coddle his son and result in an expensive report card.

We had come up against plenty of skeptical dads, but never one with this level of ingrained mistrust. To gain Bill's trust, we did something we had not done previously: We offered a probationary contract which would limit Bill's financial liability to a six-week trial. If, at the end of the six-week period, Bill did not feel that TCS was making a difference in his son's academic performance, we would release the family from the contract. Bill accepted the trial and Harry was enrolled.

Each week, we teleconferenced with Bill to find out if he saw a difference in the way Harry was handling his academic responsibilities. He admitted that he did, but noted that Harry did not spend as much time on his work as his siblings did.

We made it clear that Harry was spending the appropriate amount of time to demonstrate his understanding of the material presented. The work was meaningful, not "busy" work, we pointed out. We explained that if Harry could not complete his homework assignments, piling on more of the same would not produce an increase in mastery, but would only succeed in de-motivating him to try. Mastering his classes, we said, did not necessarily mean that Harry had to endure pain.

After following Harry's test results in his various subjects, it didn't take long for Bill to see that his son was, in fact, learning on a more than satisfactory level. Harry was earning the grades he received; no one was handing them to him. Bill soon came to understand that TCS doesn't "dumb down" algebra, chemistry, or English literature for students. What TCS does is present class material most effectively. It is a multi-faceted system constructed around a deep understanding of specific neurologies and unique learning needs; therefore, it presents material in a manner that makes sense to each individual learner.

Harry was enrolled in The Cottage School for the remainder of his high-school career. After graduation, Harry went on to a career in medical building design and construction.

OTHER WAYS TO UNDERMINE A STUDENT'S SUCCESS

Though some of the things we discuss below may seem trivial to those who have little problem operating in a mainstream world, they are stumbling blocks to unique learners and those grappling with neurological, developmental, or socio-emotional issues. Teachers and staff who are not properly trained and monitored can also sabotage student progress.

Ignoring Behaviors of Concern

Discussed earlier in both the introduction and chapter 1, The Thirteen Behaviors of Concern are integral to the TCS "For Cause" Substance Abuse Testing and Counseling Policy. All parents and students must agree (in writing) to help prevent self-medicating behavior from obscuring a student's learning and development issues and damaging the TCS program which serves all students. Prevention of substance abuse is achieved through the use of a drug screen when a behavior of concern is reported.[32]

It is vital to understand that circumventing this critical part of the TCS program makes specialized learning for the student in question unworkable. There is no judgment at play here; self-medicating simply makes it impossible for educators, parents, staff, and even student peers to know what they are dealing with, since the behavior of the student in question is under the influence of powerful substances. Equally as important is the damage to the TCS program and culture when drugs and alcohol exist unchecked in a covert subculture. Side-stepping the adherence to the policy, and not reporting behaviors of concern, compromises the student/teacher/parent partnership.

Self-medicating simply makes it impossible for educators, parents, staff, and even student peers to know what they are dealing with, since the behavior of the student in question is under the influence of powerful substances.

---

32   See chapter 10: "Resources," for the "For Cause" Substance Abuse Testing and Counseling Policy.

Not Buying Into Natural Consequences

The TCS program introduces students to real-world experiences and the real-life consequences of not playing by the rules and meeting expectations. In every way possible, our students learn that the world does not stop for them, and that, to compete and succeed in every aspect of life, they have to show up prepared and keep their commitments—or they won't get paid, won't keep jobs, won't be able to be independent and unafraid of life, and probably won't do very well in personal relationships. Mature, capable adults learn life-skills one way or another. TCS students learn these skills within our program, and thus learn to succeed even before they graduate from high school.

Mature, capable adults learn life-skills one way or another. TCS students learn these skills within our program, and thus learn to succeed even before they graduate from high school.

We've seen the myriad repercussions of not doing one's own homework, or not being able to get oneself to school on time, of one's own volition with head held high. There are any number of ways consequences can be shirked to the detriment of the student. Students, teachers, and parents must work together *consistently* to modify behavior in a positive direction. Wherever a student must learn to be responsible for his own actions, educators and parents must support that behavior and not undermine it, even if personal feelings ("I can't bear to see him struggle") dictate enabling instead. The expectation of consistency among teachers helps us detect enabling among teaching staff. When we anticipate progress with a student in a certain area and it doesn't surface, we check to make sure a teacher is not letting a student get away with something!

Even a behavior as seemingly inconsequential as forgetting to bring lunch can spawn consequences just as it would in real life. At TCS, when students bring their lunches from home, we encourage them to make their own lunches and ensure the lunch gets to school. Yet, every so often, a child forgets to bring her lunch and is unprepared to purchase the school lunch. The student's usual reaction is to feel regret, but there are other natural consequences, too: she not only misses out on gustatory delights, she must seek out some fruit or a PB&J from the school kitchen (while vowing not to make *that* mistake again!). In some instances, a parent rushes into the school office to save the day with a franchise-food lunch bag replacement.

Not so fast, we say! We explain that we will not be delivering the rescue meal to the child who forgot her lunch. "But you can't let her go hungry! She needs nourishment!" is often the reply. We then point out that no one starves at TCS, and the parent is unwittingly rewarding a forgetful child by supplying a more exciting lunch than she would have created on her own.

Incomplete Adoption of TCS

Every adult on campus has an effect on students, safety, and the atmosphere of the school. The truth is, parents and teachers alike can fall out of the school/parent/teacher partnership without realizing it, and with well-meaning if not misplaced intentions.

The Cottage School informs, involves, and celebrates each staff member to ensure the positive TCS educational experience. We live by the creed that a healthy school/parent/teacher partnership is key. But what happens, for instance, when a teacher bypasses the TCS Teacher Training Manual and makes a judgment call that sidesteps TCS? Nothing good, for behavior changes in students can only occur with *consistency* over time. Even a well-meaning teacher's actions can unconsciously serve to keep a student fettered by counterproductive behavior, instead of teaching him to soar on his own.

Example: TCS requires that each student add up his daily pay and then post his earnings in his individual check book as a deposit. The student then adds that deposit figure to the previous day's balance to determine the current balance. Each homeroom teacher is required to check the accuracy of each student's activity each day for the first two weeks of each semester. Thereafter, spot-checks suffice, as the responsibility for accuracy transfers to the student following those first two weeks of the teacher carefully checking accuracy.

But we recall one teacher who decided that two weeks of accuracy checking was overkill. Surely students would not falsify their earnings, she concluded. (And in truth, most TCS students would not.) Yet, during one routine Thursday afternoon teacher meeting (where teachers plan the student and instructor organization for the following day's "pay-off" activities), an irregularity surfaced. Three teachers noticed that one student who had not met his full pay for a few days (due to missing assignments) had elected a very expensive pay-off activity. That activity would not be affordable unless he had earned full pay on each of those days. Examination of the student's checkbook and planner revealed the student had simply recorded full pay on each day that deductions had been made for the incomplete assignments.

We all learned a lesson about the need to consistently implement the structure of TCS to ensure its success. Simply put, half measures rob students of their success.

The teacher who had decided not to carefully check her students' accounting for the initial two weeks of the semester was embarrassed to be caught diverting from the TCS teacher's manual (effective behavior modification for her, as well as her student). And we all learned a lesson about the need to consistently implement the structure of TCS to ensure its success. Simply put, half measures rob students of their success.

THE SCHOOL/PARENT/PARTNERSHIP THRIVES

Happily, the core of the staff that exists today has been integral to The Cottage School for more than twenty years. These educators and staff members have consistently maintained the TCS mission while building in innovation over time. As the school founders, we modeled and expected direct and honest communication from TCS teachers and staff; even conflict in staff meetings promotes healthy problem-solving! We know that self-advocacy, recognition, and constructive conversations are critical aspects of successful adults, such as the countless adults who have and still do form the essential TCS school/parent/teacher partnership. We *all* seek to model the positive traits that ensure our students' success.

Five Takeaways

1. **Be prepared for skeptical fathers, hovering moms, and other parental hang-ups that could detour student success.** Parents of special-needs students and unique learners grapple with exhausting challenges that, not surprisingly, can obscure clear-sightedness regarding their child's best path to success. Skepticism and over-protectiveness are classic initial reactions to TCS and its innovative approach.

2. **The Thirteen Behaviors of Concern** are the responsibility of parents, teachers, and staff. Calling out a behavior means

helping a child to succeed, not the reverse. No judgment, the TCS system cannot work when behaviors of concern are obscuring a student's actual circumstance.

3. **Understanding, preparing for, and accepting natural consequences are essential life-skills**—even if it means no fast-food lunch replacement from Mom!

4. **Yes, even a teacher can unintentionally sabotage life-skills learning.** All teachers must consistently adhere to the TCS Teachers Manual or TCS students pay the price. Empower teachers by providing opportunities for recognition, professional growth, and ownership of the school program.

5. **Partial adoption of the TCS method is non-adoption.** A scaffold tumbles when interconnecting supports go missing or are removed. The TCS program relies on an *interdependent* network of supporting members.

CHAPTER SIX

THE BUSINESS OF CREATING A SUCCESSFUL SCHOOL

Perseverance, positive thinking, and partnership-building
were our key ingredients for success.

—Joe Digieso

Looking back, we recognize that we faced endless challenges as we determined to create a brand-new school model from scratch. We had to learn the business of launching and running a school as we went. While we knew a great deal about teaching children, we were unprepared for the technicalities associated with the business of starting a special-needs school.

If it weren't for Joe's great head for business and his solid experience in business management, we might not have succeeded. Even Joe admits that every time we turned around, some new roadblock seemed to drop onto our path. It is amazing that within three years, we moved from tutoring in an office park to renting a small house, to finally purchasing a property of almost two dozen acres in the suburbs. In the first five years of operation, our student population doubled annually, making our growth exponential.

Today, The Cottage School comprises 220 students and forty-eight teachers, administrators, and staff members. This data does not include online students who—due to travel, relocation, or professional demand—receive their TCS education virtually, from points all around the nation and the world. We had no ready-made business blueprint for our success with our TCS model. But by creating our own Cottage School business and discovering what worked best, we are able to offer you the takeaways that will smooth your route to your own TCS program.

CREATING AN ACHIEVABLE BUSINESS PLAN

Our first step in building a viable TCS business plan was to ascertain if there was a need for such a school in our area. Some of our questions were:

- If there was such a need, was it too small a need to establish a school?

- Would a smaller program be better advised?

- Were there more children in the region with neurologically based learning challenges than we supposed?

- Would there be parents seeking assistance for their kids with non-neurologically based learning challenges?

- Would we be able to make it affordable?

- How would we find our students?

- How would we be able to publicize and market our unique model?

- How would we find those in the community who could contribute services, support, and the essential intelligence we needed to build our business?

Questions aside, there were three things we knew for certain:

Perseverance would be key to building a successful school business with so many challenges. We would need to believe in our cause one hundred percent to forge through obstacles we encountered.

Positive thinking would also be key to the success of our endeavor. When a goal seemed daunting or insurmountable, we would need to keep searching for solutions and have the confidence to innovate.

Partnership-building would be critical. We had to remember that it "takes a village" to ensure the success of any endeavor. We would need to gather assistance from not just the psychiatric, medical, and academic communities, but also from our targeted market community of parents and business people. Some individuals would be those with a primary interest in our school (potential families of enrollees and potential employers of graduates). Others could be those who might want to contribute to the success of the school for the good of the community as a whole. We would need, especially, to build partnerships with community members who might assist us with funding, facility and property issues, and the many bureaucratic and administrative complexities involved in launching a nonprofit, independent school program.

BUILDING A BUDGET

Fortunately, because of Joe's business background, we knew that being self-funded would be key to our upfront survival. We had to budget effectively and be able to predict our cash flow until we were well underway and had acquired a positive reputation. Additionally, we vowed never to fall into the trap of borrowing money to expand operations which, when we were watching every cent, would require large sums to service debt.

We knew that being self-funded would be key to our upfront survival.

In order to meet our funding and budget goals, we took a unique approach and involved our faculty and staff in the budget process. We empowered our faculty to manage their individual department budgets, but eliminated the "use it or lose it" mentality. We shared our fixed expenses with our faculty, including the cost for health and life insurance, social security taxes, and related employment expenses. We also shared our projections on revenue so that our people could clearly see the funds we had for department expenses.

In this manner, our faculty was intimately aware of the expenses associated with operating the school. They saw our utility expenses, telephone, and copy expenses, plus related operating costs. They knew that they had an important "business partner" role to play. Because of this, our faculty and staff understood the need to close windows when the AC was running, to turn out lights when leaving a room, to find ways to minimize the need for multiple copies of documents. They understood that they had a vested interest in assisting us with meeting our budget goals. Most teachers are very much in the dark with it comes to the hidden cost of operating a school, yet with a clear understanding of those hidden costs, our teachers developed department budgets that provided them with the materials and equipment they needed, always being mindful of the need to be as frugal as possible in order to retain funds for what mattered most.

We could go into endless detail here, but establishing the TCS budget was based on *containing* expenses to remain within cash flow. The fixed expenses such as mortgage, taxes, utilities, landscaping, maintenance, staff and teacher salaries, and weekly food and beverages had to be painstakingly detailed. Importantly, research had to be conducted to uncover additional items we might not have anticipated: licenses, registrations, government fees, etc. We also had to accurately predict monthly income.

We were fortunate that one of us was a business pro, familiar with financial planning for new ventures. Educators and parents interested in launching a special-needs or other type of independent school program don't always have financial-planning experience. Our word to the wise: bring on a financial consultant with nonprofit experience.

Having said that, even with the best possible budgeting assistance, you may find—as we did—it was what we did not know about launching a nonprofit independent school that tripped us up, exposing us to expenditures we had never anticipated. There are many rules regarding the physical, logistical, and regulatory requirements of nonprofit enterprises. We had assumed that Joe's financial experience in (for-profit) business would fully extend to our new nonprofit venture, and we were surprised to find out all we did not know. So, bring on the certified financial help and check first to ensure that

It was what we did not know about launching a nonprofit independent school that tripped us up, exposing us to expenditures we had never anticipated.

your consultant is well-versed in nonprofit school startups in your state, county, and city.

A positive note: when you have constructed a solid and realistic budget, it is a good deal easier to raise money for a brick-and-mortar (facilities construction or renovation) campaign.

ATTRACTING FUNDING AND SUPPORT

In the beginning, we admit that we had little time to think about funding because we were focused on creating a program that worked, adhering rigorously to our self-funded budget, and getting the word out to attract students. Later, we crafted a funding approach that first looked at already existent sources.

Uncovering Vouchers, Scholarships, and Other State Programs

When we began TCS, there were few financial resources beyond individual donors and financial grants. Today, any school can explore federal, state, or local governmental funding to find available money. Many states offer a voucher system, which can be a win-win for students and schools alike.

In 2007, the Georgia legislature passed the Georgia Special Needs Scholarship Program, allowing qualified independent schools to receive state funds for students served under an IEP. Vouchers soon became an important source of taxpayer funding for independent special-needs education in Georgia. And there were additional public dollars to which we could direct our applicants: the national EdChoice website[33] details funding options for virtually every state.

---

33   "Types of School Choice and How They're Funded," EdChoice, accessed March 25, 2019, https://www.edchoice.org/school-choice/types-of-school-choice.

If your state does not effectively meet funding needs for unique learners, do as we did: partner with other independent schools (yes, even your competition!) to create a better voucher system model. Then, sell that revision to your state legislators.

Partnering with Other Independent Schools

Although the assumption may be that independent schools are fiercely competitive, the atmosphere in the Atlanta area is one of partnership, and that may be the case in your area as well, so check out local, state, and national agencies.

Our local agency (the Atlanta Area Association for Independent Schools), the state agency (the Georgia Independent School Association), and the national agency (the National Association of Independent Schools) provide vital resources and opportunities for partnership. In our case, local participating school partners had the wherewithal to bring in nationally and internationally recognized authorities for a two- or three-day event targeting parents and professionals of students with unique learning styles. Together, we subsidized the consultants' travel and expenses and hosted staff development opportunities as well as public informational seminars. Hundreds of people attended to find out what we were doing and how we were changing education and the community for the better. These events helped to raise awareness and catapult the reputation of our participating schools into the forefront.

Meetings revolved around a single topic such as: how to teach math to dyslexic students; how to monitor social media use for special-needs students; and how to work with Tourette's or OCD[34] learners. Attendees loved the seminars that included a look at the

---

34   Obsessive-compulsive disorder

latest assistive technologies: devices to help manage children's social media use, new voice-recognition programs designed to accommodate non-readers or non-writers,[35] and text-to-voice pen readers.[36]

Multi-sponsored informational events for the community are always highly effective ways to demonstrate just how valuable and funding-worthy special-needs education is.

They were excited to see real-life demonstrations of non-writing students effectively dictating a written assignment or a story they had conceived. Even today, something new to help special-needs learners is around every corner, and multi-sponsored informational events for the community are always highly effective ways to demonstrate just how valuable and funding-worthy special-needs education is.

Often, we would acquire sponsorships from the participating vendors. If our event was about dyslexia, for instance, we would seek out sponsorships from providers of compensatory tools, methods, or research. Those funds might be used to defray the expenses of the event itself (effectively making it a no-cost event to the schools involved). Or, we would distribute the funding among the sponsorship schools, to seed the next event. Other partnering options would include hosting job fairs and offering relevant films for community viewing. Our partnerships provided exposure that attracted both students *and* donors.

In order to market the events, we contacted our local and state associations of independent educators to secure email links and list services. We sent event announcements to other schools in the area,

---

35   The first Dragon Naturally Speaking, for instance: https://www.nuance.com/dragon.html.

36   Such as Pen Reader: http://www.readerpen.com.

region, and state, and added our events to calendars and organizational alerts.

We also sent out press releases to local civic groups. School parents were happy to drop our event announcements at Rotary and Kiwanis associations, and at local women's clubs. We reached out to local newspapers, always including compelling visuals and background info with our event writeups. Our school partners even secured public service announcements and interviews on local radio and TV stations. Today, a strategic social media campaign is doubtless your most effective marketing tool.

Partnering with Public Schools

We also partnered with public schools—a decision that may have made administrators of other independent schools uncomfortable. (Don't forget, the independent school movement began generations earlier as a reaction to governmental control. Historically, independent school administrators are wary of accepting government funds.)

Although we founded an independent school, we support public school systems that do the very best they can with overwhelming student numbers, innumerable regulations, and limited funding. No single school system can meet the needs of all students, as public systems are charged to do. Our previous experience in the public sector working with families of special-needs kids taught us that many times, litigation issues cropped up between at-risk student families and their public schools. Soon after opening our doors, we began working with counties, seeking solutions for "problem" students who were costing the public school system a great deal of money. And since every student at TCS has an IEP, the partnership process was streamlined.

Public schools embroiled in conflict and facing litigation soon determined that it would be less expensive for them to pay our tuition and avoid a lawsuit altogether. Our first high school student, for instance, had been diagnosed with Tourette's and his school had been compelled to hire an additional full-time teacher to be with him at all times. That teacher's annual salary was much more expensive than our (at the time) $15,000 tuition expense. In addition, the situation had become embarrassing for the student, who felt isolated and awkward.

As it turned out, the quid pro quo of working with the county schools was extremely beneficial to us, the public schools, and to the families of our unique learners. We acquired many more referrals directly from the public school system. Ironically, though the schools often believed they were sending us an unfixable problem, because of our unique system, we were able to provide a successful solution for the school, student, and family and a win-win-win partnership situation. If an alliance became difficult, we simply withdrew from it.

The quid pro quo of working with the county schools was extremely beneficial to us, the public schools, and to the families of our unique learners.

Gifts, Grants, Angels, and Business Partners

It's crucial to know how to use your school's successes to attract donors, angels, business partners, and grants. This kind of funding and support involves people who are behind the scenes, supporting the school financially, but not directing or influencing the operation, growth, or mission of your school.

Interestingly, most of our angels have been attracted to The Cottage School because of our unique model of using a business milieu to prepare our students for a world in which they will succeed. Time after time, our angels have been business and commerce members who are extremely successful and involved in the community. They have told us often that our mission reminds them of the struggles, intimidation, and failures they or their family members experienced during their own school years. Their reaction to The Cottage School is generally, "I wish I had known about a school like this. How can I help?"

Not long after we launched, we recognized that if we were going to grow, we needed to be out there *telling* people how they could help. That meant school leadership and parents needed to be actively engaged in spreading the word. So, Jacque moved out into the community and spoke with everyone possible. Eventually, that role was passed on to a marketing and community development individual, but until that could happen, Jacque spoke to business groups everywhere in our region. She met with, and was invited to, public schools to talk to parents about how they could get their children to do homework, or how they could develop good relationships with their children's teachers. Wherever she went, whenever someone said, "And what do you do?" Jacque was ready with her ninety-second "elevator" speech, and it almost always prompted people to ask more questions. She went to events and served on every committee she could find. She joined the Chamber of Commerce, the local Leads Club ("Connect, Collaborate, Prosper") and other leadership groups such as our local Roswell Women's Club. When she gave a talk or interacted, Jacque always provided an introduction to our program to anyone with interest in The Cottage School—not just prospective families.[37]

As we began to approach foundations, we learned that it was the more sophisticated enterprises, or those with well-established track records, which received funding. That was especially true for those with prominent backers or missions of broad philanthropic appeal (battered women and homeless veterans, for instance). Still, we visited foundations that matched our needs, invited them to visit our campus, and looked for potential personal connections to foundation staff or board members. Although we were perceived as new kids on the block, by the time we were ready for our first capital campaign, we received a major financial grant for capital improvement. While the majority of our donations represent individual gifts, our foundation partners have been most generous in supporting us in capital improvement campaigns.

It is important to note that any nonprofit 501(c)(3) organization must adhere not only to the rules established by the IRS, but also to the ethical standards established by the Association of Fundraising Professionals.[38] Regardless of the source, school administrators must always clarify donor and school expectations *in writing.* Otherwise, donors may assume they have the right to direct school policy, influence acceptance/rejection of applicants, or hold sway over organizational decisions. An independent school—especially one for unique learners which relies on a highly specialized structure—does not want to accept dollars with strings attached that could negatively impact mission and success.

---

37   See chapter 10: "Resources," for a recent example of a TCS handout.

38   Association of Fund-Raising Professionals, accessed March 25, 2019, https:// afpglobal.org.

In 1985, for instance, we experienced a classic example of a gift with strings when a neighbor offered us $100,000 to ensure our enrollment would not exceed seventy-five students. That sum was monumental to us and we doubted at the time that we would ever enroll more than seventy-five students. However, even for a huge donation, we were not willing to hand over influence to an individual interested only in controlling the neighborhood by imposing restrictions upon us. We did not accept his donation and, as it turned out, we ended up with a great deal more than seventy-five students!

As for business partnerships, we wanted to be sure that companies knew what we were doing so they could help us with direct funding, in-kind donations, or job placement opportunities for our students. Early on, through her meetings with business leaders, speaking engagements, and participation on committees, Jacque found plenty of in-kind assistance for us. She first befriended a communications technology leader who made sure our students had cutting-edge technology. Then she brought in local banks to sponsor the checks and checkbooks that form the

> **Even for a huge donation, we were not willing to hand over influence to an individual interested only in controlling the neighborhood.**

basis of our Pay Level program. She even found a manufacturer to supply our students with backpacks and attracted a firm to set up our school recycling program, gratis. TCS parents routinely assist with in-kind business donations such as landscaping, special campus events, and the signage needed for events.

Finally, when it comes to building relationships with any angels, grantors, business partners, or donors, it is essential to recognize donations in a manner beyond the traditional thank-you letter. The Cottage School routinely expresses gratitude by publishing recognition of support in local publications, spreading the word via social media, making announcements at school and community gatherings, and deploying signage at special events. The more recognition a donor receives, the better.

Think strategically. You, too, can launch a tutoring or educational business that will serve as market research or supply needed revenue. There are plenty of additional part-time and supporting ventures that can serve dual purposes for your TCS program, as well. Think strategically! Instead of selling wrapping paper, choose a revenue-generating or gratis venture that will also help you build your client base. Then get the word out via the Chamber of Commerce and other community assistance groups.

Offer school psychologist and/or educational testing services. You will need to partner with such resources anyway, why not consider bringing them in-house and working out a mutually beneficial arrangement? Recent graduates in these areas may be especially open to the prospect, and while a revenue stream can be split, the partnership will boost exposure for both the school and the in-house professional.

Rent out your facility to bring students and resources to your door. What is your facility earning on weekends or during holidays and summer months while you are paying the mortgage and utilities? By renting out the campus, you can bring in people who will become aware of and intrigued by your mission—and who will spread the word. We have rented our facilities for teacher training classes, camps, special events, and more. In the process of boosting revenue we greatly expanded reach.

Offer free meeting space to help special-needs groups. For so many reasons, we felt it was important to offer free meeting space to any learning disability groups or agencies. When the regional Tourette's Syndrome Association needed a conference venue, for instance, we offered up The Cottage School. We did not collect fees, but welcoming regional parents greatly increased our exposure to new students—a win-win for all.

Make your buses available for nonprofit events. Aside from making our venue more attractive for use by including free transportation, it certainly never hurt us to have philanthropically minded people traveling on Cottage School buses. They appreciated the good will and were more likely to remember us come pledge-drive time.

Send your best salespeople (your students!) into the community. Our students consistently volunteer for, or participate in, community events, inspiring high regard along the way. During the annual Roswell's Women's Club home tour, for example, our students served as tour guides. They also participated in community fairs where our carpentry class built local agency concession stands and then helped to sell goods. And our students volunteered to clean or helped set up temporary housing for homeless families. Some of these activities are devised as mini-businesses; others are strictly volunteer-based. Either way, our poised, friendly, and knowledgeable TCS kids are our best advertisement.[39]

---

39   Our students love to share what the TCS program has meant to them. See "How The Cottage School Has Helped Me" in chapter 10, "Resources."

HIRING AND INTERVIEW POINTERS

As we've so often mentioned, our tutoring business was essential to the launch of our bona fide school. One reason: it gave us access to some of the best schoolteachers in the area—our own tutors! We already had sound relationships with teachers who were skilled, interested in working with unique learners, and successful at it. We simply asked, "Would you like to come and work with us at The Cottage School?" We consciously looked for diversity in age, ethnicity, culture, and gender; it has always been critical for us to seek demographic balance across our staff. Because of our work building relationships with local educators and institutions and our profile in the region as a unique place of learning for special-needs students, we did not hire headhunters or used professional placement agencies. Often teachers approached us around the time that the new contracts went out in February.

> **Our tutoring business was essential to the launch of our bona fide school. One reason: it gave us access to some of the best schoolteachers in the area—our own tutors!**

The TCS interview process is a key aspect of building a strong faculty. Not only do candidates interview with a supervisor, but prior to a final hiring decision, they must interview with their prospective team. Obviously, background checks and well-considered, probing questions ("What do you like most about your career or current job?") are important. To reveal teaching style, we have always looked for *concrete* accounts of daily situations, not adjectives. For instance: "Describe a class experience that you felt was most successful for your students" is always more effective than "How would you describe your teaching style?"

The Cottage School seeks teachers who are attracted to, not annoyed by, student questions or those students who require more time than others. TCS needs teachers who are not set in their own philosophies and methods but are open to, and consistently exploring new ideas. Candidates should express excitement at working with the school age they would be assigned. The interviewer watches for tell-tale signs of rigidity that would not work at The Cottage School: "I don't do this," or "Don't ask me to do that." And we try hard not to unwittingly elicit such statements through our own ill-considered actions. We've never, for instance, asked an instructor to teach a subject in which he or she was not comfortable ("We know you're a science teacher, but this semester we need you to teach art …").

Finally, attitude has always been as important in our teachers as it is in our students. Attitude forms an essential rung of our school scaffold and culture. Over the years, we have parted ways with candidates who had the needed skills but not the caring and consistently committed attitude we seek.

SPACE AND LOCATION

Whether you are a group of parents thinking about setting up a cooperative TCS program, or a group of individuals considering the launch of a bona fide TCS facility, researching the availability of affordable and suitable school space in an accessible location is key. That research should eventually cover all options, and you should expect outreach and ongoing in-depth discussion to be a solid part of the process.

Will your space initially be donated, rented, or a shared communal space for smaller programs? Many co-ops launch in a member's home or place of business, if unused space is available.

Small schools often work well in shared community facilities, such as places of worship. Consideration should always be given to starting small and then moving to larger and more expensive space only as enrollment demands and supports.

Consider bringing a financial and nonprofit consultant to the space-and-facilities discussion, even if you think you will be setting up for three students in someone's home. There may be tax, legal, zoning, and nonprofit filing requirements to consider, and you will need to be aware of them earlier rather than later! Eventually, you may wish to consult a nonprofit-focused commercial real estate specialist, as well. Note: It is always helpful to have the assistance of a (free) parent consultant, so check for the aforementioned skills among your target family community.

GROWING A BUSINESS

To juggle the growth of any TCS program, you must learn to be a "business whisperer!" Joe's best advice is to always start small and move to larger and more expensive space only as enrollment demands and supports. What you're aiming for is growth balance: you don't want to expand ahead of your revenue stream and projections (remember our own "no loan" proviso). On the other hand, if you wait too long to expand your space, you will effectively be "under-growing," or jamming too many students and staff into the facility. This could possibly impact your revenue as families and staff go elsewhere because of overcrowding or the sense that your school is not well-managed or successful enough to provide adequate facilities and resources. In growing any business, there is always that element of risk: expansion versus revenue. At a certain point, a well-considered leap of faith is needed to prod you to seek another space in which to house your venture. Basically, you'll know it's time to look for a new location so that you can expand—but in a *profitable* mode.

Allow your school to become a little tight first, because you may be launching a capital campaign of some sort to help fund your expansion or move. You will want your parents to be aware of the need for more space! That awareness will help them financially support you as you mount your capital campaign. Try to think ahead: Strategically manage your requests for financial assistance so that your solicitations for donations are not competing with each other. Our approach was to resist *aggressively* growing our TCS business. Rather, we believed in being business "whisperers" who would listen to what our school was telling us. We let it grow *us*.

Five Takeaways: Ace the Business of Creating a TCS School

1. Budget, don't borrow. If your school and other (part-time and supporting) revenue streams can't support your fixed and projected expenditures, revisit your launch equation.

2. Look for funding where it already exists—vouchers, in-kind, individual donors, alternate revenue sources, and grants.

3. Partner with other independent schools to lobby for better legislation and create powerful community events that will raise your profile in the region.

4. Partner with public schools and local businesses to effectively build school population.

5. Become a business "whisperer" to grow your nonprofit special-needs school safely and effectively.

CHAPTER SEVEN

LEARNING FROM OUR STUDENTS: THREE EYE-OPENING STORIES

Finally, someone knew how my brain worked! My TCS teachers understood that I needed to draw in class so that I could sit still long enough to take in the lessons. They "got" that I wasn't behaving poorly, I was simply using my own special way of paying attention.

—Serena, a TCS student

Parents and educators reading this book will doubtless wonder as they work through previous chapters, "TCS sounds like a great model for our own school initiative, but will it work for *my kid(s)?*"

Our answer is an unequivocal yes! The TCS structure provides the kind of experiential rewards-based instruction and culture that could only arise from the deepest understanding of learning challenges. Much of that understanding comes from immersion in constantly evolving research and in intensive training. Yet so much of the

TCS program is constructed not just upon what we, as instructors and professionals, know and bring to the table. A great deal of the TCS program was, at its inception, built upon what we learned from our students—what our students taught us.

We utilized our years of previous experience working with unique learners to devise the TCS program. To this day, it remains an outstandingly effective program. Yet, undeniably, one of the great strengths of TCS is that, as teachers, we are always looking for the endless ways to reach our students. In fact, one of the most important things we learned is that *every student teaches the teacher*. (You can check out the other five lessons we learned from unique learners in the box at the end of this chapter.)

One of the most important things we learned is that every student teaches the teacher.

So, while the scaffold of our TCS program is as integral as it ever was, over the years we have added classes, electives, and other effective rewards and experiences to help our students keep moving enthusiastically forward in their quest to succeed. For thirty years, we watched and assessed what brought the light into students' eyes, for we knew if something worked for one child, it might work for another as well. Along with our own innovative ideas such as the Pay Level system and clocking in and out, we have always been open to hearing what our students have to say. So each and every year, we try out student suggestions that we suspect may be helpful to one or one hundred. Many times, the suggestions work; sometimes they do not. We try them anyway!

The best way to demonstrate the success of the unique TCS program over thirty years (with students presenting the broadest constellation of challenges imaginable) is to share some of our students' own stories.[40]

SERENA'S STORY: LET THE ARTIST THRIVE AND LEARN

When Serena came to us for her initial ninth-grade entrance interview, the first thing we noticed was that she was a young woman with an artistic sense of style. Her Tourette's syndrome was not immediately evident.

"I've loved art for as long as I can remember," Serena told us, her dark eyes shining as she spoke of her passion for any form of artistic creativity. Her expression dimmed when she recounted experiences that had plagued her all through her school years. "I can't tell you how often I got into trouble for drawing during class," she said. "I never could stop my creative thoughts or resist the urge to start drawing right then and there, no matter what kind of instruction was going on."

> "I never could stop my creative thoughts or resist the urge to start drawing right then and there, no matter what kind of instruction was going on."

Serena pointed to other behavioral issues, as well, including invisible "storming" (a symptom associated with Tourette's syndrome). Serena would appear to be day-dreaming when, in fact, she was experiencing a neurological "storm" which, as it ended, would leave her no longer connected to what had transpired immediately prior. In addition, she was impulsive verbally and behaviorally. Unable to resist artistic and neurological impulses, Serena struggled

---

40   We have changed the names of our case study individuals to protect their privacy.

with failure throughout her early school years. Her teachers were at a loss to deal with her behavior; fellow students were perplexed and wary. Serena and her parents knew she was "different," yet they didn't know what to do about it. Serena became more and more defeated and felt increasingly isolated. Her innately sunny disposition often turned morose.

When Serena was nine, she was finally diagnosed with ADHD and Tourette's syndrome. Still, by middle school, "trying to pay attention in a traditional classroom had become nearly impossible for me," she admitted. She continued to fail.

Then, before she could continue on a downward trend in high school, her parents brought her to The Cottage School. At TCS, Serena remembers, "The administrators and teachers got to know me personally. Finally, someone knew how my brain worked! My TCS teachers understood that I *needed* to draw in class so that I could sit still long enough to take in the lessons. They 'got' that I wasn't behaving poorly; I was simply using my own special way of paying attention."

The educators and consultants at TCS had not only been trained to recognize Serena's particular neurologically based learning challenges, they had extensive hands-on experience with students who faced similar (although always personally unique) challenges. The TCS model of experiential learning, with its consistently supportive scaffold structure and safe school culture were, in fact, designed for students just like Serena who had self-developed exceptional behaviors or needed to uncover such means to help them learn.

Serena happily sketched her way through her TCS classes and learned at a pace and in a manner mapped out in her IEP, and thus designed to work specifically for her brain.

Serena happily sketched her way through her TCS classes and learned at a pace and in a manner mapped out in her IEP, and thus designed to work specifically for her brain. She graduated salutatorian of her class which "gave me the confidence to go into the world as an adult," she happily reports.

No surprise to anyone, Serena chose art as her career path. She also graduated with a degree in business administration from Georgia State, picked up a paralegal certification from Kennesaw State along the way, and has authored two books. Having learned to open life's options, Serena ensures she will always have more than one opportunity to take advantage of.

MARK'S STORY: RESCUE A "SYSTEM-DAMAGED" UNIQUE LEARNER

Mark, diagnosed with autism, was socially less mature than his classmates and often exhibited self-stimulating behaviors. Somehow, he had made it through to fifth grade at a local inner-city elementary school, before he hit a wall he could not surmount. When Mark and his parents came in to our offices for a sixth-grade admissions interview, we learned that Mark was a gentle, well-liked student who had managed to carry on in a mainstream setting even when his peers could, at times, be cruel. Then (his mother's words, not ours) "Mark met the proverbial teacher from Hell who terrorized, berated, and demeaned children."

Like many parents, Mark's mom and dad simply didn't realize the extent of the damage Mark had sustained under his fifth-grade teacher until after the school year ended. While chatting with other class parents at the local pool, while the kids swam and enjoyed the first days of summer, they learned that many of the children had been victimized by an educator not equipped to instruct students, let alone to instruct those with learning challenges.

"Mark needs a place to regroup, get his confidence back, and continue on his learning path after all the disruption," his father explained. Understandably, he and his wife were hesitant to advance Mark to the local middle school. "We knew that whatever his learning and social issues were, it would be better for him to be in a school where educators were trained to understand those issues and embrace them. The Cottage School was a perfect fit."

At TCS, Mark was able to work within a framework of consistent routine, preparation, and expectation so essential to his ability to learn. Though his interactions often remained immature, his demeanor was so gentle that TCS peers and staff alike enjoyed his company. Mark grew more independent and confident every day.

"Mark's first year was incredible," his parents told us some time later. "His American History teacher ignited an excitement for learning he still retains," they said. Mark's TCS reading instructor not only helped him master his comprehensive reading, she is Mark's Facebook friend and cheerleader even today. According to Mark's parents, all ten of his TCS teachers contributed to his social and educational success and left a lasting and positive impact on their son. How different might his middle- and high-school careers have been had he remained in his local school system? "I don't know how The Cottage School improves the lives of children; it just does," Mark's mom has written to us. "At The Cottage School, all children are better for the experience."

As for Mark, he went on to graduate magna cum laude with a degree in business and hospitality from Beacon College in Florida. He also spent a remarkable college semester in Italy. Today, Mark is pursuing a successful career in hospitality and has a happy and rewarding life.

GEORGE'S STORY: GENTLY REWIRE FOR CONFIDENCE AND SUCCESS

From his earliest memories of school, George struggled to learn because he could not discern the words that everyone else seemed to read easily and he couldn't remain attentive to things he wasn't able to understand. George's dad had grappled with his own dyslexia and attentiveness challenges. The last thing he wanted was to watch his son endure the crushing difficulties he himself had faced as a boy, long before anyone even knew that dyslexia existed.

> **George's dad had grappled with his own dyslexia and attentiveness challenges. The last thing he wanted was to watch his son endure the crushing difficulties he himself had faced as a boy.**

George was enrolled in an Atlanta private school for students with reading disorders, where he managed to hold his own right up to eighth-grade graduation. Academics had continued to be a battle, but he was an attractive and engaging young person who made friends everywhere he went. Along the way, George discovered other diversions, too: He loved animals and he enjoyed growing things. He also developed a passion for carpentry, working on any projects he could get his hands on. (He even transformed his parents' back door into a Dutch door, albeit without permission.)

The private school did not continue past eighth grade, so George began his freshman year at the local public high school, while his parents hoped for the best. At the end of his third week in ninth grade, George came home from school one day and suffered a serious meltdown. Distraught, he admitted that he hadn't been able to understand anything that was going on in the classroom. He was completely overwhelmed. George's parents knew about The Cottage School program, and they brought him to us directly.

The carefully structured, rewards-based TCS program was just what George needed to achieve academic success. With every good grade and positive result, he beamed with pride. Although academics were never easy for him, he worked diligently toward expectations on a realistic schedule, approached his landmarks step-by-step, and met the goals he had devised with the support of his mentors. Rewards-based experiential learning encouraged him to succeed academically while he simultaneously pursued his innate talents and developed valuable life-skills. (George did not have to "forego" his extracurricular joys to focus solely on his academics. He simply had to make sure he earned them each day by meeting the goals he himself had set.) The TCS culture and structure were just what George needed. His carpentry and other talents expanded exponentially as his academic foundation strengthened.

The TCS culture and structure were just what George needed. His carpentry and other talents expanded exponentially as his academic foundation strengthened.

After George graduated from The Cottage School, he purchased several acres of rural property, built his own house from the ground up, and secured some local home-building contracts. His one stumbling block: George was afraid to take the qualifying exam for the local construction profession, for fear he might fail. Besides, he said, the work he delivered was of such high quality that his lack of credentials did not seem to get in his way. At The Cottage School, however, he had learned that with determination and realistic goals, he could achieve almost anything. He simply had to map out his expectations and goals, and tackle them one-by-one with a plan, on a schedule that would work for him.

A few years later, (with plenty of building and carpentry success to his credit) he faced his fears and took the test. We will never forget his elation when George contacted us to let us know he had passed the dreaded qualifying exam for his business! Today, George has the life he always dreamed about. He and his wife live on a small farm where he tends to his garden and animals as he also pursues his rewarding construction career.

What Our Students Have Taught Us: Six Takeaways

One of the secrets behind the TCS program success is to learn what unique learners need from those learners themselves. The following revelations, gleaned from our work with thousands of young people, are those upon which our program was constructed.

1. **Every child wants to be successful.** We learned early on that no matter how much a student might protest, or how incorrigible he or she may seem, (and we've seen incorrigible) all young people want to succeed.

2. **Every child has talents and strengths.** Yes: *Every* child has talents. Children who are encouraged and appropriately schooled go on to become math professors, chefs, horticulturists, or excellent parents. Others open dog-walking businesses or art centers, become physical therapists, or build houses. It only

matters that each becomes an independent and confident adult who can make his or her own way in the world. Given the opportunity, each child will find at least one passion, calling, or pastime to serve them well. Many discover multiple interests and develop skills around each. So, be a "child whisperer" and *listen* to what your young people are trying to tell you about who they are.

3. **Every child requires a safe environment in which to develop.** No child (or adult, for that matter) can flourish in a toxic or detrimental environment. Carefully consider culture or milieu when you seek a learning environment for your special-needs— or *any*—learner. A gardener can't grow flowers in acid and the same goes for young learners: they will not thrive or grow in a caustic or counterproductive culture. If your children are describing a school environment where they cannot be heard, take note! If they are not succeeding, suspect the worst and seek safety.

4. **Every child builds success** on strengths, not weaknesses, just as happy, productive adults build lives and careers on strengths. Nothing is served by overlooking strengths that already exist in favor of focusing on what might be considered weaknesses.

5. **Every child needs inspiration to achieve goals.** If we all thought of goals as bicycles without pedals, and pedals as the inspiration needed to keep bicycles moving forward, it would be easier to comprehend why pedal-less bicycles don't get very far. It is not enough to help a child set a goal, educators and parents must help to ignite the energy that will be needed to achieve the goal. If the bicycle analogy does not work for you, think: How far would you travel in a new car if you had no

access to gasoline or electricity? Then think about your own life-long interests and passions: Who initially introduced you to them? How did they inspire you to keep pursuing your passions even when things got rough?

6.   **On their journey, every child teaches their teacher.** Lessons from students are ever-present and only go unheeded if they are unheard or unseen. Pay attention! See and hear the messages your students are sending you about how they learn best. If you do, not only will you teach that student well, you will develop a rich and dimensional portfolio of methods and techniques for all the students yet to come before you.

CHAPTER EIGHT

LAUNCH YOUR OWN TCS PROGRAM

The mind is not a vessel to be filled, but a fire to be kindled.

—Plutarch[41]

Anyone determined to bring a new educational mind-set to special-needs *or* mainstream learning should heed the words above, attributed to the Greek (and later, Roman) biographer and essayist Plutarch.[42] In his *Parallel Lives* and *Moralia*, Plutarch wrote about the virtues and vices of notable personages of his day, but his larger concern was for the strength and survival of both the Greek and Roman cultures. He valued the careful nurturing of thought and knowledge intrinsic to the persistence of those civilizations. Looking again at the chapter quotation above causes us to wonder: Would Plutarch have considered much of today's education in America "fire-kindling?" Or would he have termed it "vessel-filling"?

---

41   Jona Lendering, "Plutarch," Livius, November 2018, https://www.livius.org/articles/person/plutarch.

42   Ibid.

In more modern terms, these are the questions many parents and educators are asking themselves in the twenty-first century as they assess the education their children are receiving. With the rapid growth of the home schooling and co-op school movements,[43] it's clear to see that many parents are not completely satisfied that American education is dedicated to kindling the fires of their children's minds. With the mandate to meet state educational and curriculum standards in order to receive funding (public schools) or competitively move as many students as possible on to higher education (private schools), educators are understandably focused on imparting a predetermined volume of knowledge to fill up the little vessels that sit before them each day.

Unfortunately, the *individual* student and the uncovering of his or her personal strengths, interests, and passions may be lost in the crush of conventional education mandates. What's more, today's brand of academically driven education does not necessarily prepare students to become contributing, accountable, and responsible adults in the world beyond school. It does not always serve to ensure that young people will be the workers of tomorrow that employers seek. And it may not help to create young people who

---

43   Home schooling, for instance, is estimated to be growing seven times more quickly than the rate of public school enrollment, according to Bright Hub Education.
Caroline Timone, "The Growth of the Homeschooling Movement: More Families Than Ever Choose to Homeschool," Bright Hub Education, 2019, https://www.brighthubeducation.com/homeschool-methodologies/p128233/.

can confidently succeed in their adult lives, even if they succeeded in school.

What can parents and educators do to help deliver education better balanced for the real world—education that is responsive to the unique learning needs of each student? How can schooling better serve to ignite each child's passion for learning, exploring, and succeeding in the world beyond school?

PROVIDING THE MISSING LINKS IN MAINSTREAM EDUCATION: RELEVANCE, MANAGEMENT, SELF-ADVOCACY, AND CONSEQUENCE

Clearly, we believe that the TCS model of real life-based, experiential learning supplies the missing links of *life-skills learning* that is so badly needed in education today. These links include

- learning that is **relevant** to students and their lives;

- instruction that embeds the kinds of study and life **management** skills essential to growth;

- an educational milieu in which students are encouraged and trained to appropriately express their needs and **advocate** for themselves; and

- most importantly, an education and a learning culture in which students gain a true understanding of **consequence** for actions, and learn how to manage action versus consequence.

Relevance. We have spent our careers (and the past seven chapters of this book) devoted to creating relevant education that helps each child realize his or her strengths across academics, the arts, sports, leisure activities, and more. It is an educational environment that, by seeking out the relevance to each child's strengths, augments mainstream education to stoke a passion for learning and discovery. A TCS education sends young people out into the real world independent and confident, open to new experiences and lifelong learning.

Management. The work-milieu scaffold of a TCS education allows students to integrate the life-skills of handling their own problems, and challenges such as time, project, and problem management, rather than relying on external sources and cues for those essential actions.

Self-advocacy. TCS also teaches students to become self-advocates by effectively negotiating for what they need or believe is fair and helpful. One way they do this is through their creation of their own Individualized Education Plan or IEP, as we have demonstrated earlier in this book. But the TCS culture consistently encourages and reinforces this skill.

Consequence. Above all else, everything within the TCS environment is designed to instill the importance and power of consequence. Many of today's parents and educators know intimately just how disabling it is for young people to embark on adult life and work without self-assuredly managing the consequences of their actions, whether those actions are positive (growing small successes into larger ones) or negative (foreseeing the results of potential missteps). It is constantly reaffirming for us to know that the consequence-management skills our TCS kids practice day in and day out travel with them into the everyday workplace. We hear all the time from employers who tell us they are amazed that a young person fresh out of high school can handle responsibilities so maturely. We know

> Everything within the TCS environment is designed to instill the importance and power of consequence.

those consequence-management skills will not only promote our students' success in the workplace, but will contribute to a happy life in general, free from unnecessary fear of the unknown.

MODELING TCS: TIPS FOR ADMINISTRATORS AND EDUCATORS

Before you begin to devise plans for any TCS initiative, check out our sampling of tips for educators and administrators below. And if you are contemplating the introduction of a TCS initiative within an existing public or private school, why not work in two or three of the following suggestions first, to get a sense of the far-reaching change possible through a bona fide TCS initiative?

Support each student by focusing on a strength. Teachers often don't realize that they get too busy to say something nice or supportive to the quiet student, the kid who is always failing, or the one who is trying to fade into the linoleum. But every teacher can mention something positive that they notice or something a child has done well. Every child—especially a fragile special-needs learner—thirsts for support. When other things are going wrong, if they hear, "That was a very polite way for you to talk to Sam," or, "Thank you for sharing today," they may feel empowered to keep at it. Every student needs to hear something they can feel good about, especially when the challenges are so great.

Intentionally connect with each student. Meeting the challenge described in the tip above this one is much easier for teachers (and administrators, too) if they *intentionally* connect with each student. At The Cottage School, when the bell rings at the end of class and students are moving about, each teacher is already at the door instead of at his desk finishing up paperwork or the like. All of our staff members, in fact, are trained to meet and greet or say goodbye at the door. They understand the trepidation and self-consciousness each student may feel in class ("I'm the only one falling behind!" or, "Why can't I learn like the others?"). So, each student is welcomed with a smile, a greeting, and eye contact (if the child can manage it). The point is: the teacher intentionally connects with each child.

This kind of effort has always proved critical in the real world, as well. For centuries, pastors have connected with each member of their flock by meeting and greeting at the entrance to the church. And in *The One Minute Manager*,[44] a perennial bestseller, authors Kenneth H. Blanchard and Spencer Johnson advise managers to make sure they connect with as many employees as possible each and every day. That purposeful connection is a statement of confidence and faith that assures each worker that her role is important and her presence within the company is valued.

Seek opportunities for students to interact in a philanthropic manner. In decades past, smart teachers, administrators, and parents understood that children benefitted greatly from the core life lesson of utilizing their own skills or knowledge to assist within their communities. With the help of TCS administrators and teachers, TCS students routinely get out of the classroom to apply subject knowledge they have acquired to tutor or aid others, to assist the homeless, to help build housing or other needed structures, or to simply help out at community functions. The ability to be philan-

> **The ability to be philanthropic and aid others is a life skill that helps the helper as much as those helped.**

---

44   Kenneth Blanchard and Spencer Johnson, *The One Minute Manager* (New York: William Morrow and Company, 1982).

thropic and aid others is a life skill that helps the helper as much as those helped.

Connect with parents regarding their children's strengths. TCS teachers and administrators don't wait until a child is in trouble or a parent is upset to connect with parents. The TCS model ensures that communication patterns are established to relate more of the *positive* than the negative. At the start of the school year, our teachers and administrators find ways to communicate to parents how special their child is, and that they are getting to know and appreciate their child's strengths. And when a relationship is first grounded in acceptance and positivity, it's that much easier to make a difficult call down the pike.

"Trickle down" a positive, supportive teaching environment. How an administrator interacts with teachers, staff, and other administrators—plus the supportiveness of the systems that the administrator establishes—all send a strong message. After all, if a TCS administrator wants a teacher to support students, he must first demonstrate that he always has her back, too.

Administrators who are overly critical and quick to undermine teachers often jeopardize student accomplishment as well as educator success. Too many administrators are simply "too busy" to spend time in the classroom or with their teachers, and only step in to troubleshoot. Too many teachers report that they do not feel connected to their head of school. They don't feel like the headmaster knows them, understands how they teach, or appreciates their innovation in the classroom.

But TCS administrators are focused on personally knowing each of their teaching staff, understanding their strengths, and supporting their educators in every way possible. The message is: "You're an important part of this school. I like the way you teach and I like *you*.

You've done a good job with this student." The message to parents thus is: "I know this teacher. I watch him at work every day. I can respond to your concerns with personal knowledge of this teacher's work." The TCS administrator purposefully creates, nurtures, and adjusts the culture as needed for all members of the TCS community, including the pivotal roles of each teacher.

Teachers must be open to objective assessment. Even the most well-meaning educator has faced a class of test scores that indicate no one understood the material. In cases where a preponderance of students are not progressing, a teacher must be open to having message and effectiveness assessed, and be willing to accept responsibility for lessons that weren't very effective, or instructional concepts that didn't make lift-off. In the business world, that's called quality control. Don't take it personally! A TCS administrator connected to her teachers follows classroom results, knows when things go off the rails, and can help with needed guidance. Correspondingly, a TCS educator fixes whatever is needed to get the job done well.

Create a communication system that builds trust within the teaching and administration staff. Somewhere along the way, most teachers and administrators have experienced a school environment wherein administration or teachers disparage other teachers under the radar, not tackling issues in a straightforward manner. Subversive behavior can unravel a teaching staff in a heartbeat, resulting in a toxic environment of cliques and turf wars. In such milieus, teachers not only become less effective educators, they communicate an unsafe environment to the children, just as quarreling parents do inside a home.

At The Cottage School, the teaching and administrative staff meet weekly to share vital information about students. These meetings also give voice to internal issues that need to be addressed and empower teachers and staff members to find their own solutions—just as TCS students learn to advocate for themselves and problem-solve in their Pay Level meetings. What's more, because TCS mandates close, effectual communication and regular, in-class visitation between the head of school and each teacher, under-the-radar toxicity is virtually eliminated.

Encourage teachers to promote innovation and creative classrooms. When an administrator promotes innovation, she rewards teachers in the same way teachers should reward their students—by encouraging them to use their innate and learned skills to problem-solve and think outside the box.

> **Because TCS mandates close, effectual communication and regular, in-class visitation between the head of school and each teacher, under-the-radar toxicity is virtually eliminated.**

Provide opportunities for team building. TCS administrators seek out channels, notably social activities, that will help teachers and staff to get to know each other, appreciate each other's value, and discover common bonds. Such activities might take time away from or extend a typical work day, but TCS administrators know that political and emotional issues arise when teachers don't know or appreciate each other or even their own strengths and how they contribute to the team. The truth is, a self-focused "professional" environment does not necessarily promote a healthy educational environment. Teachers who team with and learn to find value in what others can bring to the table model for their students what the working world will expect of them: that they will be expected to interact, serve on committees, and complete projects with individuals they may have assumed they would not like, understand, or appreciate.

MODELING TCS: THREE ESSENTIAL POINTERS FOR PARENTS

Parents who wish either to support a TCS initiative in their child's current school environment, or launch a TCS homeschooling or cooperative initiative, should be committed to the following pointers for best results:

Parents should establish a positive communication system with teachers early on. This is paramount whether you are introducing TCS change in your child's current school environment, establishing your own or group TCS initiative, or assisting in a TCS school launch in your area. Because parents know their child best and know more about their child's learning style than a new instructor, they need to make a concerted effort to meet with their child's teacher in a non-threatening way to discuss mutual expectations for the student(s). Then, ask: What does the teacher expect from the parent? What can the parent expect from the teacher? How can parents best communicate about the students—their aspirations, interests, strengths, and concerns? The first TCS parent-teacher meeting can even be a quick let's-get-acquainted opportunity or a polite clearance call about delivering cupcakes to the class. You don't want early miscommunications to lead to "problem parent" or "unresponsive teacher" branding!

Students must complete their own assignments! Parents who "help" their children by doing their homework for them make it impossible for teachers to assess a student's needs. Yes, it's confusing for parents who, within mainstream education, only wanted to protect their children from being tagged as "stupid" or being demoted from

> **Parents who "help" their children by doing their homework for them make it impossible for teachers to assess a student's needs.**

one class to another. But remember: The TCS program *exists* to make learning possible for unique learners, to help them complete their studies in a way that works for them—not for their parents. A parent needs to ensure that the student has a quiet, non-chaotic place to study that is conducive to learning. And it is a parent's role to set appropriate study hours and to serve as a study buddy if a child asks, "Will you go over these words with me?" or "Will you read my paper and see how it sounds?"

Keep parents informed. Uninformed parents are non-participatory parents. Some parents complain that their school does not reach out to families effectively. At the same time, other parents groan that they drown in the endless outreach from multiple teachers, administrators, and other sources as each week progresses. Persistent missives can be ignored and, consequently, balls get dropped.

As headmaster of The Cottage School, Jacque was sensitive to these issues in her quest to ensure parents were informed but not overwhelmed by school communications. Every week, coordinated messages from teachers, administration, event planners, and professional experts, were aggregated in a single weekly outreach to parents, enabling them to quickly scan and synchronize planning for the week ahead. Today the communication goes out via an e-blast. For those parents helping to launch any kind of TCS initiative—homeschooling, co-op, embedded/blended program, or brick-and-mortar TCS school, the word must go out to parents: *Stay informed!* To assist your child's TCS-based education, participate!

CAN'T CHANGE YOUR EDUCATIONAL MODEL?

Six Ways to Introduce a TCS Educational *Environment*

At community gatherings, when we meet parents and educators frustrated by the roadblocks they face within their state educational systems, Joe always reassures them that they don't have to slay a giant to help their children succeed. He says: "You may not be able to change the educational *model*, but you can change the educational *environment*."

Short of moving to Roswell, Georgia, and enrolling your child at The Cottage School, how can parents and educators secure more effective education for special-needs or mainstream students in their own locale? Our answer: with careful planning and expert assistance, if needed, they can introduce a TCS educational *environment in any of the six following ways, to start.*

1. **Offer TCS training**. Introduce the TCS philosophy and life-skills learning within a public or independent school, via teacher and administrator seminars and training.

2. **Suggest a TCS try-it-out program**. Introduce the TCS philosophy and life-skills learning within a public or independent school via a school-year pilot program, exploratory initiative, or summer camp program.

3. **Find out about the school-within-a-school concept**. Introduce the TCS philosophy and life-skills learning within a public or larger independent school, via a school-within-a-school program. This concept has been experimentally deployed in large, public high schools

especially, over the past two decades. The US Department of Education even offers funding to qualifying schools seeking to embed smaller learning communities. To find out about pros and cons, Google the concept or refer to this article from The Education Resources Information Center. [45]

4. **Start small with home-schooling or a co-op**. Many parents who have seriously thought about home-schooling may consider launching a custom-sized TCS co-op or home-schooling program for one or a group of students. It is an ideal solution, combining the best of TCS experiential learning with the ability to control a bite-sized initiative.

5. **Launch a "blended" TCS co-op or home-schooling program**. Taking step #4 above one step further, blended programs utilize contracted conventional classes for specific classes and activities such as science labs, physical education, technology instruction, and more. This approach can provide new home-schoolers with access to broader-spectrum education for their children, while helping ease the instructional load.

6. **Launch a full-scale brick-and-mortar independent TCS-based school**, just as we did. This book is a great way to start thinking about the many considerations involved.

---

45   The Education Resources Information Center (ERIC) is an online digital library of education research and information. ERIC is sponsored by the Institute of Education Sciences of the United States Department of Education.
Tobin McAndrews, and Wendell Anderson, "Schools within Schools. ERIC Digest," The Education Resources Information Center, accessed March 26, 2019, https://www.ericdigests.org/2002-4/schools.html.

LAUNCH TO SUCCEED: ELEVEN LESSONS LEARNED

When we founded The Cottage School back in 1985, Jacque said the following:

> *"If we really want our school to work, we're going to put in the hard time and we're going to do it the hard way, because that's what works. When you start taking shortcuts to make it easy on yourself, you miss an opportunity to impact a child."*

We know that is why The Cottage School works when other programs fail. If you are considering home-schooling your own special-needs child in an experiential, life-skills-learning environment, or you are an educator or administrator thinking about launching a TCS school or a program for both mainstream and special-needs students, remember these lessons learned:

1. **Keep lessons experiential.** We can't say it more plainly: Most young people, especially unique learners, learn by **what they** *do,* not by what they listen to in class. Delivering lessons only via lecture may be easier for the instructor, but it's not what works for the learner.

2. **Start with simple, achievable goals for students:** getting to school on time, dressing appropriately for school, bringing required materials, using appropriate methods of communication, completing the tasks at hand. These simpler goals not only introduce the model for more complex goals, but once internalized through consistent repetition they wire young brains for *all* goal achievement. As these skills become innate, they also free up human decision-making RAM.

3. **Always keep the focus on what is in the best interest of the student.** Again: "*When you start taking shortcuts to make it easy on yourself, you miss an opportunity to impact a child.*"

4. **Keep parents informed along the way.** Be willing to discuss situations with them that will allow the school and parents to be on the same page.

5. **Parents' work *begins*, not ends, with the partnership with the school.**

6. **All must pay the initial cost of behavior modification plans:** student, teachers, parents, family members. *Everyone* must be willing to pay the consequences of change, and change their own behavior, as needed.

7. **All must be willing to make commitments** and sacrifices of time, stress, and finances.

8. **"Natural consequences" education requires hard work** and parents' and teachers' true understanding of "loving" behavior toward students. A parent does not demonstrate loving behavior by continually dropping off a child's forgotten lunch bag. The hard work requires *not* delivering the lunch so that the child learns to take care of himself.

9. **Layer program structure for students and teachers as the community evolves.** For example, add funding for more extracurricular or leisure-time activities, team-building, continuing education, etc., as finances strengthen. Increase community involvement as the school community evolves.

10. **Never stop brainstorming innovation!**

11. **Celebrate the successes** internally, to the student and teacher community, to parents and families, and to the outside community and the world at large. Remember to use your successes as effective "marketing" content for collateral, websites, etc.

Your Own TCS Initiative: Five Takeaways

1. **Relevance, management, self-advocacy, and consequence** are the missing life-skills links that TCS supplies to augment and transform conventional education.

2. **Always keep the focus on the student!**

3. **Teach experientially.** It's not about adhering to a lesson plan, it's about *learning*.

4. **Pick your launch mode.** Don't just think brick-and-mortar school: a TCS Initiative can exist within an existing public or private school in any number of ways, or can launch as a standalone co-op or institution (see the previous box, "Six Ways to Introduce a TCS Educational Environment").

5. **Administrators, teachers, and parents alike must be well-versed** in the TCS model, and must learn to communicate in new ways, to ensure success.

CHAPTER NINE

WORKING WITH CONSULTANTS

Sometimes, asking for help is the most
meaningful example of self-reliance.

—Unknown

Certainly, working with an expert—someone who has "been there and done that"—is a great deal easier and more time-efficient than constantly re-inventing wheels. When we searched for the chapter quote for this closing chapter, however, we were also tempted by this one, from Danish physicist Niels Bohr (1885–1962): *"An expert is a man who has made all the mistakes which can be made, in a narrow field."*[46] We are, after all, disciples of mistake-making and all its benefits! The fact is, though we were confident of our many years of research and field work with unique learners, we also learned so

---

46   "Niels Bohr Biographical," The Nobel Prize, accessed March 26, 2019, https://
www.nobelprize.org/prizes/physics/1922/bohr/biographical/.

much from what we didn't know: namely, the mechanics of how to launch a nonprofit, brick-and-mortar, special-needs school.

We were fortunate that Joe had a great deal of business background, and we were blessed to have benefitted from what we saw as others' missteps in their own special-needs program design. So, a business plan and a vision for program design were not our stumbling blocks. But in launching a bona fide school, we certainly faced many others.

HOW TO KNOW IF YOU NEED HELP

Yet what if you are a parent considering a TCS homeschooling initiative for a small group of local students? Googling "home schooling" in your state will provide you with endless resources: information about state laws, local and regional homeschooling associations, Department of Education rulings and guidelines, other co-operatives and homeschooling academies, books, videos, and more. And a well-credentialed homeschooling consultant can cut through much of the mumbo-jumbo for you, making your goals feel a good deal less daunting and even accessible. You may need only a session or two to help you get started. It's all about time saved and (sometimes costly) missteps avoided.

> A well-credentialed home-schooling consultant can cut through much of the mumbo-jumbo for you, making your goals feel a good deal less daunting and even accessible.

What if you are part of a group of parents and educators ready to find or build a school facility to house a nonprofit, state-accredited, TCS school? What kind of guidance should you seek? Which experts or consultants will be most valuable to you? How should you search for them? Which part of the project should you attack first? Which parts next?

Even if you are a parent determined to pitch the idea of embedding a TCS program within a local public or private school, how should you present that concept? You might guess that the more complete and well-researched your TCS school-within-a-school proposal, the more likely it is to be taken seriously by a local public or private school. Yet, how do you go about formulating a convincing presentation that may only have one shot to be heard? Where can you find the guidance you need?

Items discussed in this book, such as developing a business plan, conducting target market research in your area, potential for group or community support, managing potential obstacles to viability, creation of mission and culture, selecting a leadership team, creating a budget, sourcing funding, hiring and training, and (if one is needed) locating a site, are all essential to consider for many TCS initiatives. But you may have other questions, as well: "Do we need a Board?" "What is our personal or group liability?" "How will we know what size property to consider for a brick-and-mortar school?" And don't overlook the concern we always considered from as many angles possible: "What could go wrong with our TCS initiative?" (We have a more informed answer to that question now than we did thirty years ago!)

YOUR PROJECT STARTING POINT: WHAT TCS GUIDANCE BRINGS TO THE TABLE

If you are reading this book, then you, too, are concerned about the quality of today's educational systems. Sometimes it seems that we are stuck in constructs that have long outlived their purposes.

Think about such outmoded ideas in the adult world: Do businesses succeed when employees memorize the data they need, stay in one place to receive information, or work on projects that rarely receive feedback? The workplace has learned that success relies on vision and innovation; education must benefit from this insight, too. For, clearly, when it comes to schooling, there is work to do to prepare our youth for their best lives.

Certainly, there are excellent educators in classrooms around the world, and effective educational systems delivering services to students. Yet, too many students are left behind, overlooked, or suffer the denial of their dreams. *These children have talents!* The success of our TCS model is an undeniable testimony to the hidden talents of many underserved students, and to the positive impact of an experiential, behaviorally-based program.

The potential to change your school environment is within your reach. Because all educational growth begins with an assessment, we welcome the opportunity to assist in ascertaining your particular needs. After an initial assessment, TCS consultants can help determine how the TCS program would be appropriate for your initiative. More detailed data on community needs and resources will help determine if an entire school program is viable.

We hope this book has provided a road map for exploring new educational possibilities. Our goal: to help interested parents, educators, and administrators reconfigure their educational environments to serve all learners.

For more information, query us at joed@cottageschool.org or jacqued@cottageschool.org

CHAPTER TEN

RESOURCES

EXHIBIT A: THIRTEEN BEHAVIORS OF CONCERN

1. Abrupt changes in mood or attitude.

2. Sudden and/or continuing decline in attendance at school.

3. Declining level or performance at school.

4. Sudden and continuing resistance to proper discipline at school.

5. Difficulties or changes in levels of peer relationships.

6. Stealing.

7. Excessive secrecy about actions and possessions.

8. Frequent conversations which seem preoccupied with drug use.

9. Possession of drugs or alcohol or drug paraphernalia.

10. Excessive sedation or excitement.

11. Unsteady gait.

12. Odor of alcohol or other illicit substances.

13. Exchange of money.

EXHIBIT B: "FOR CAUSE" SUBSTANCE ABUSE TESTING AND COUNSELING POLICY

In order to implement a policy that can serve to help control the use of drugs and alcohol among our school population fairly, without infringing on individual rights unnecessarily, The Cottage School staff offers these guidelines:

1. The Cottage School believes that the prevention and diagnosis of adolescent substance abuse should primarily be the concern of the adolescent, the parents, and the family's physician. The Cottage School advises parents to consult their physician regarding substance abuse concerns and/or use of the adolescent urine drug screen program based on the Cobb Country Medical Society model, which is available at a number of metro Atlanta hospitals.

2. The Cottage School Substance Abuse Screening Program offers a second line of defense to help TCS students stay drug free and thus protect both the student and the school, while also assisting those parents who are afraid to confront a possible drug abuse issue with their own children. A TCS **Authorization for Drug Screening** must be signed by enrolling parents and the student to complete student enrollment.

3. No student will be required to have a drug screen or saliva alcohol test run without reasonable suspicions of substance-using behavior. In the presence of one or more of the **Thirteen Behaviors of Concern (see Exhibit A),** and in an effort to determine if substance abuse is affecting the student, the school will

   a. obtain a supervised saliva and/or urine specimen from the student, which will be tested for illicit substances,

   b. inform parents of this action and of the behaviors exhibited, and

   c. develop a plan for addressing the student's problem.

4. The Cottage School staff recognizes that some Behaviors of Concern also signal other problems not related to drug or alcohol use. Therefore, the alcohol or drug screen will serve as only one aspect of our problem-solving approach, and may be coupled with required participation in professional counseling without continuing drug screening.

5. School personnel will want to receive permission from parents to have periodic consultation with the counseling professional(s) selected by the family.

6. Failure to comply with any aspect of the problem-solving plans outlined by school personnel may result in termination from the school program without consideration of refund.

EXHIBIT C: THE COTTAGE SCHOOL THIRTY-YEAR ANNIVERSARY INFORMATIONAL FLYER

Building a sense of self for students with special learning needs through academic and experiential programming, The Cottage School prepares individuals for fulfillment of their true potential as confident, productive, and independent adults.

Welcome to The Cottage School, where we have been nurturing students with special learning needs in grades six through twelve for over thirty years. From our beginning as a one-room tutoring center with a one-of-a-kind educational program for unique learners, we have grown to a dedicated staff of fifty who educate over 170 students, using both indoor and outdoor classrooms spread throughout the school's twenty-three-acre campus. Located along the Chattahoochee River Corridor, the schools boasts a cutting-edge media center, an arts and athletics facility, and a trail system suitable for both mountain biking and cross country.

In June of 2014, The *Masters in Special Education Resource Guide named the Cottage School one of its* **Top 50 Best Special Needs Schools in the United States.** One reason we were selected is our innovative approach to teaching and learning which includes

- **a balanced blend of academic and experiential programming**, wherein students develop the confidence and skills to delve into academic, athletic, artistic, and social endeavors that they may once have felt were out of reach;

- **a highly qualified faculty with a low student/teacher ratio** of 10:1, to accommodate various learning styles and allow for differentiated instruction;

- **a variety of unique and innovative learning techniques**, including a highly effective time-management system; and

- **seventeen offered sports at the varsity, junior varsity, and middle school levels**, with a "no cut" policy for non-varsity sports that enables all students to participate in the sport(s) of their choice.

In today's highly competitive world, success can mean many things. At TCS, *we ensure success by providing each student the tools and confidence necessary to pursue his or her chosen postgraduate path.* What's more, we work with each student to develop an individualized post-secondary plan for success. Our curriculum meets Georgia's graduation standards as well as requirements for the HOPE scholarship.

Please visit us online at cottageschool.org to learn more about what makes The Cottage School such a wonderful place to grow and learn. Better yet, visit us in person and see how we are preparing students for success.

We look forward to hearing from you!

EXHIBIT D: "HOW THE COTTAGE SCHOOL HAS HELPED ME"

What do TCS students themselves say about the education they have received? The following is a sampling of quotations from middle and high school students at The Cottage School.

"TCS didn't only prepare me for college, it prepared me for life."

"I like the small classes because it helps me learn more and get individual help, which I hardly got in public school. I also like the exploratories such as art, hiking, horseback riding, golf, photography, and mountain biking."

"One way this school has benefited me is that my grades have gone from F's to A's and B's. It has improved the way I act and how I put effort into what I do. I did some history work and the teacher was so proud of what I had done, he told just about everyone he knew. My social life has improved. I have at least six close friends that I can trust. Last year the only way I could keep my friends was to do what they did."

"This school has brought out a little of the positive side of me. The school also helped me find out what things I'm good at. The teachers show me easier ways to get the answer. I'm lucky to have teachers like them. I think this is the best school I have ever been to."

"The good thing about The Cottage School is that it helps prepare me for life and supports me. The structure holds me responsible for my actions. Just the way the school works helps me. I've learned to take risks because of the feedback. I know that I have to make a difference in this world, thanks to my friends. I also plan to take even more risks and gain confidence in myself!"

"At my other school the teachers did not really care about what you did. They gave you the homework and if you didn't do it, oh well. [At TCS] I like the reward system because it makes me work toward a goal at the end of the work and it takes my mind off the work."

"The Cottage School has helped me in many ways. This school has an awesome way of teaching. Classes are more interactive and hands-on. I've learned how to wrestle and throw a discus. I can finally do a pushup and I can jog without losing my breath."

"[At TCS] they don't yell at you when you do something wrong like they did at my old school. The teachers love us. I have grown to like this school. It has helped me socially, emotionally, and in some ways, spiritually. I am hoping it will teach me important skills I will need in the long run."

BIBLIOGRAPHY

American Psychiatric Association. Diagnostic and Statistical Manual of Mental Disorders (5th ed.). Arlington, VA: American Psychiatric Publishing, 2013.

Blanchard, Kenneth H., and Spencer Johnson. The One Minute Manager. New York, NY: William Morrow and Company, 1982.

Boyington, Brianna. "See High School Graduation Rates by State." US News & World Report. May 2018. https://www.usnews.com/high-schools/best-high-schools/articles/2018-05-18/see-high-school-graduation-rates-by-state.

Cox, David. "A Learning Disability Often Makes for a More Visionary, Innovative CEO." Quartz. May 2015. https://qz.com/413783/learning-disability-makes-for-a-more-visionary-innovative-ceo/.

Dynarski, Mark. "Is the High School Graduation Rate Really Going Up?" The Brookings Institute. May 2018. https://www.brookings.edu/research/is-the-high-school-graduation-rate-really-going-up/.

Fried, Hilda, and Sally Liberman-Smith. Plain Talk About Children with Learning Disabilities. Rockville, MD: Dept. of Health, Education, and Welfare,

Public Health Service, Alcohol, Drug Abuse, and Mental Health Administration, National Institute of Mental Health, Division of Scientific and Public Information. 1979.

Fry, Richard. "It's Becoming More Common for Young Adults to Live at Home—and for Longer Stretches." Pew Research Center. May 2017. http://www.pewresearch.org/fact-tank/2017/05/05/its-becoming-more-common-for-young-adults-to-live-at-home-and-for-longer-stretches/.

Lendering, Jona. "Plutarch." Livius.org. November 2018. https://www.livius.org/articles/person/plutarch.

Love, Dylan. "15 CEOs with Learning Disabilities." Business Insider. May 2011. https://www.businessinsider.com/ceo-learning-disabilities-2011-5.

McAndrews, Tobin, and Wendell Anderson. "Schools within Schools. ERIC Digest." 2019. https://www.ericdigests.org/2002-4/schools.html.

Nadeau, Kathleen G. *ADD in the Workplace: Choices, Changes, and Challenges.* London, England: Routledge, 1998.

National Research Council. *How People Learn: Brain, Mind, Experience, and School: Expanded Edition.* Washington, DC: The National Academies Press. https://doi.org/10.17226/9853.

"Niels Bohr Biographical." NobelPrize.org. Nobel Media AB 2019. https://www.nobelprize.org/prizes/physics/1922/bohr/biographical/.

Orr, Linda M., and Dave J. *Eliminating Waste in Business: Run Lean, Boost Profitability.* New York, NY: Apress Books, 2014.

Page, Libby. "How to Deal with Employability Anxiety." The Guardian. May 2014. https://www.theguardian.com/education/2014/may/19/ employment-anxiety-students-job-worry.

"The 50 Best Private Special Needs Schools in the United States." The Masters in Special Education Program Guide. Accessed March 7, 2019. https://www.masters-in-special-education. com/50-best-private-special-needs-schools/2014/.

Timone, Caroline. "The Growth of the Homeschooling Movement: More Families than Ever Choose to Homeschool." Bright Hub Education. 2019. https://www.brighthubeducation.com/homeschool-methodologies/ p128233/.

"Types of School Choice and How They're Funded." EdChoice. 2019. https:// www.edchoice.org/school-choice/types-of-school-choice/.

Wolff, Barbara, and Hanyana Goodman. "The Legend of the Dull-Witted Child Who Grew Up to Be a Genius." The Hebrew University of Jerusalem. February 2016. http://www.albert-einstein.org/article_handicap.html.